EMPOWERING IT PROFESSIONALS

Career Trends and Skill Building for the Digital Age

Unleash Your Potential and
Stay Ahead in IT Career

MOHAN V BORGAONKAR

ISBN
Paperback 979-8-89610-722-4
Hardcase 979-8-89673-311-9

!!Dedication!!

This Book is Dedicated to Our B10 Family Group

My Parents – Dr Vijay, and Mrs Anuradha – Nurture me

My Spouse and Children – Mrs Manjiri, Sneha and Shreyas –
Motivate me

My Brother and his family – Milind, Mrs Mrunal,
Shruti and Sushrut – Support me

!!Cheers!!

Contents

Preface

At present, the IT world is at a threshold of one other major technological revolution, which may change the way of working for IT Professionals, and the User Experience, how the business functions are envisioned and implemented. The IT Professionals find themselves in this 'ChakraVyuvh' or Labyrinth state, with Continuous Change and Innovation driving the industry.

The Book "Empowering IT Professionals - Career Trends and Skill Building for the Digital Age" is thought of, with a deep understanding of the challenges and opportunities that define this dynamic field. As technology changes the IT world at a rapid pace, the need for IT professionals to stay ahead in their careers has never been more critical. And it will always remain ever-demanding.

This Book is designed for IT Professionals, to act as a comprehensive guide, at all Career stages; whether you are a fresh Graduate seeking an entry into the industry; a Senior Experienced Professional aspiring for advancement in a career with Managerial Or Leadership birth; Or someone stuck up between career steps; and for the Executives, as a ready handbook to guide the reporting people Or new entrants; the strategies and insights presented here will help you traverse the complex and rapidly changing IT Industry landscape.

In essence, the book provides two strategic aspects viz. It is understanding IT career trends and building essential skills. We drill into the latest trends that are shaping the present and future of IT, from Traditional IT to Latest technologies like Artificial Intelligence, machine learning, Cybersecurity, Cloud computing, Gen AI and Quantum. Adopting these trends, allows you to anticipate industry trends and prepare yourself strategically for future opportunities.

Along with IT career synthesis, this book emphasizes skill-building as a critical component of Career Development. Technical skills are very much required, but soft skills such as Communication, Leadership, and Analytical skills are equally important. The right weightage of these skills defines your performance and your ability to lead and drive in a technology-driven world.

Throughout this book, you will find practical advice, real-time examples, and strategies to adopt. Each chapter is crafted to provide you with the knowledge needed to thrive in your career. We explore formal education, certifications, hands-on experience, and networking, elaborating on how each element contributes to your professional growth.

"Empowering IT Professionals - Career Trends and Skill Building for the Digital Age" is more than just a book; it is a roadmap and essential guide for navigating the future of IT. By investing in your career development, you are not only enhancing your prospects but also contributing to the advancement of the overall industry in totality.

I invite you to embark on this journey along with me. Let's explore the exciting opportunities that are coming up and unlock the full potential of your IT career. Together, we can build a future, where technology serves as a Catalyst for Innovation and Success.

Yours Sincerely,

Mohan V Borgaonkar

From the Author's Desk

Inspiring Foreword

If you've ever considered the ever-evolving landscape of the IT industry and how to thrive within it, then "Empowering IT Professionals - Career Trends and Skill Building for the Digital Age" by Mohan V Borgaonkar, is your essential guide. This book delves into the key trends and skills necessary for success in a rapidly changing field, equipping you with the insights needed to navigate your career path.

As a Mind Performance Coach and the author of the bestseller "Unleash the Power of Reading," I understand how self-awareness and personal growth can profoundly impact your professional journey. In a world filled with technological advancements and constant distractions, do you find it challenging to maintain clarity in your career goals? "Empowering IT Professionals" offers valuable insights to help you regain control over your thoughts and ambitions.

In today's fast-paced environment, the pressures of the industry can often cloud your vision. This book serves as a guiding light, empowering you to take ownership of your career and navigate the complexities of the IT world with confidence and purpose. The journey it presents is not just about skill acquisition; it's about understanding your values and leveraging them to build a fulfilling career.

Throughout the book, practical strategies and insights will be shared, offering tools to enhance your technical abilities while also cultivating essential soft skills like communication and leadership. These tools will empower you to filter out the noise and focus on what truly matters in your professional life.

Whether you're a recent graduate eager to make your mark, an experienced professional looking for advancement, or someone contemplating a career transition, "Empowering IT Professionals" is here to support you. If you're ready to embrace the opportunities ahead and unlock your full potential, this book is your indispensable companion on your journey to success.

Best wishes,

Dr. Manjunath M.S.

Mind Performance Coach and Author of "Unleash the Power of Reading"

Chapter 1

Introduction

In the fast-evolving realm of Information Technology (IT), continuous career development is essential for long-term success. As the digital landscape changes, IT professionals must prioritize innovation and adaptability. This book, "Empowering IT Professionals - Career Trends and Skill Building for the Digital Age," serves as a comprehensive guide to help navigate and thrive in this dynamic environment.

The Importance of Career Development in IT

The rapid growth of the IT industry, coupled with constantly evolving technologies, necessitates continuous education and the adoption of new skills. Career development in IT encompasses formal education, certifications, skill badges, practical experience, and collaboration. Each element plays a crucial role: education provides the foundational knowledge needed, certifications validate and enhance skills, hands-on experience connects theory with practice, and networking and collaboration open up growth opportunities.

As industries increasingly rely on technology, the demand for skilled IT professionals continues to rise, leading to numerous job opportunities and attractive salaries. However, to capitalize on these opportunities, IT professionals must stay updated with the latest skills and knowledge. If they do not, they risk becoming obsolete in an ever-evolving technology landscape.

Career development fosters personal growth and job satisfaction. Continuous learning improves professional competence and cultivates a sense of achievement. It enables IT professionals to stay ahead of industry trends, anticipate future challenges, and position themselves as invaluable and irreplaceable assets.

This book examines the trends that are shaping the IT industry and provides strategies for developing essential skills. It covers everything from emerging technologies to important soft skills such as communication and leadership. The upcoming chapters will prepare you for a successful career in IT, regardless of whether you are just starting or looking to advance. "Empowering IT Professionals - Career Trends and Skill Building for the Digital Age" serves as your comprehensive guide to excelling in this dynamic field.

Investing in your professional growth boosts your career prospects and contributes to the evolution of the IT industry. Let's thrive on this journey together and unlock your full potential in IT!

Navigating the Rapid Changes in the Digital Age

In today's fast-paced IT landscape, technological change is occurring rapidly. For IT professionals to stay relevant and competitive in the industry, it is essential not only to adopt current changes but also to anticipate future trends and prepare for them.

The bottom line for the adoption of technological change is a commitment to continuous learning. The traditional model of 10+2+3-4 years of formal education and relying on it as a base for further career is not viable. And Career Long Learning is required in various ways.

a. Organizational Mandated Training and Certifications: The various Organizations have mandatory training, badges and certifications, based on the Industry Needs. These skill updates are essential for the Companies and the Individual to sustain and cater for the upcoming/ ongoing Industrial business requirements.

b. Open Market Courses and Certifications: Various training Platforms and Institutes like Coursera Plus, Udacity, and Udemy offer courses on the latest technologies and methodologies. Pursuing Certifications in the latest technology areas like cloud computing, cybersecurity, and data science can provide a competitive edge.

c. IT Industry Workshops and Conferences: The IT Industry level workshops and conferences on various Ongoing strategic topics are conducted by well-known Institutes and Personalities. This allows the professionals, the opportunity to learn from experts, collaborate with peers and seniors, and stay well acquainted about the latest trends and topics.

d. Membership of Professional Institutes and Communities: The professional organizations and online communities, such as GitHub, Stack Overflow, and PMI, offer various trainings and Certifications, along with networking avenues with conferences. This can foster continuous learning and provide support from a network of Subject matter experts.

Develop Agility and Adaptability

In a rapidly changing environment, agility and adaptability are essential traits. IT professionals must acquire new skills, tools, and processes, and adjust to any upcoming roles and responsibilities. This will require personal drive with:

a. Always Remain Well Informed: Regular reading of industry publications, blogs, and research papers helps professionals stay updated with technological advancements and industry shifts. A Rapid Reading habit can be developed, and it can help grasp more knowledge in a shorter time.

b. Explore and Innovate: Adopting a mindset of exploration and innovation can lead to the identification of new solutions and approaches. This can be facilitated by exploring stretch projects, participating in Challenge competitions, or contributing to generic open-source projects.

c. Furnish Soft Skills: Enhancing soft skills such as analytical skills, problem-solving, communication, presentation skills, negotiation and leadership is essential for navigating change. These skills enable professionals to manage uncertainty and challenges, lead teams through transitions and steady states, and effectively communicate the implications of new technologies or the Change itself.

Proactive Career Management

To remain in control of own career path is vital in the digital age. It is always better to have proactive career management. This would involve:

a. Set Right Career Goals: Clearly define your short-term and long-term career goals. This helps professionals stay focused and motivated. Also, regularly reassess the goals concerning industry changes and ensure they remain relevant.

b. Build a Personal Brand: Establish a strong personal brand through Thought leadership, Active contribution to social media platforms, speaking engagements, and a professional online presence. This can enhance visibility and career opportunities.

c. Collaboration with Networking: Build and maintain a healthy professional network. The Networking can lead to mentorship opportunities, job referrals, and collaborations that might not otherwise be openly accessible.

Leveraging Emerging Technologies

Understanding and leveraging emerging technologies is crucial for staying competitive in the digital age. IT professionals need to remain vigilant at all times. Here are some actions to consider to keep up with industry standards:

a. Track the Emerging Trends: Keeping eyes and ears open for emerging technologies such as blockchain, quantum computing, and Gen AI. It helps professionals anticipate future directions and prepare themselves accordingly.

b. Align to Strategic Approach: Assess how emerging technologies can be applied strategically within the organisations to drive productivity, optimisation, innovation, efficiency, and competitive advantage.

c. Continuously Reskill / Upskill: Proactively acquire skills related to emerging technologies and ensure that professionals are ready to implement and manage these innovations efficaciously.

Conclusion

Navigating the rapid changes of the digital age requires a multifaceted approach that incorporates continuous learning, agility, proactive career management, and the strategic use of emerging technologies. By embracing these strategies, IT professionals can adapt to change and position themselves as leaders and innovators in the constantly evolving technological landscape.

Objective of the Book

The primary objective of this book is to serve as a comprehensive guide for IT professionals and those aspiring to enter the field. It outlines the IT career path and the skills necessary for success. With this knowledge, IT professionals can navigate their careers confidently, even amidst the inevitable changes in the industry—since change is the only constant.

This book provides pathways for educating IT professionals, offering insights into the evolving IT industry and emerging technologies. It highlights current career trends and opportunities effectively.

Additionally, the book offers methods for identifying essential skills and guides on how to acquire them. It includes practical advice for career progression and transitions. The book also features insights into the journeys and achievements of notable figures in the IT industry. Furthermore, it presents an overview of key technologies and their impact on opportunities for IT professionals.

Essentially, this book will assist IT professionals in successfully navigating the IT industry and serve as a comprehensive resource for essential career steps.

Chapter 2

Career Trends in IT

We should examine the history of the IT industry and how it has evolved over the years and centuries. It is interesting to note that the initial growth of the industry was very slow. However, with the current pace of change, the growth is now occurring at a rapid pace.

Brief History of IT

The journey of the Information Technology (IT) industry truly began in the 20th century with the advent of modern computers. In the 1940s, the first electronic computers were developed. During the 1950s and 1960s, mainframe systems became the predominant technology for large corporations and government agencies. The introduction of the World Wide Web in the 1990s revolutionized how information was shared and accessed, leading to a significant boom in IT careers, such as web development, network administration, and cybersecurity. Although the dot-com boom spurred remarkable growth and innovation, it was followed by a crash that underscored the volatility of tech markets.

From the 2000s to the 2010s, notable advancements occurred in mobile technology, cloud computing, and social media. Today, IT has become an essential function across all industries. The rise of generative AI, machine learning, blockchain, and quantum computing is shaping the future of technology. IT professionals now work in various fields, including healthcare, finance, entertainment, and education. Emerging roles such as AI specialists, cybersecurity experts, and data analysts are in high demand, reflecting the evolving landscape of the IT industry.

Overview of Current and Emerging IT Career Trends

In today's rapidly evolving digital landscape, change is the only constant. The Information Technology (IT) sector epitomizes this relentless pace of innovation and transformation. Just a few decades ago, the internet was an emerging technology, cloud computing was only a futuristic concept, and the idea of artificial intelligence seemed limited to science fiction. Fast forward to the present, and these technologies are not only real but also integral to our daily lives and businesses.

As an IT professional, navigating this dynamic environment requires more than just technical skills. It demands a keen understanding of the trends shaping the industry, the foresight to anticipate future developments, and the agility to adapt to new roles and responsibilities. Whether you are a seasoned veteran or a newcomer to the field, staying ahead of the curve is essential for maintaining relevance and achieving career success.

This chapter explores the current and emerging trends in IT careers, providing a comprehensive overview of in-demand roles, essential skills, and the technological advancements that are driving change. We will examine the rapid growth of data science and cybersecurity, as well as the transformative potential of quantum computing and blockchain technology.

By understanding these trends, you'll be better equipped to make informed career decisions, identify growth opportunities, and strategically position yourself in the fast-paced IT landscape. Let's embark on this journey together and discover the future of IT careers, ensuring that you not only survive but thrive in the digital age.

The Rise of Remote and Hybrid Work Models

The workplace has seen a significant transformation in recent years, primarily due to technological advancements and changing cultural attitudes toward work. The COVID pandemic accelerated these changes, prompting organizations and employees to adapt to new working methods. While most IT organizations still prefer traditional office settings for all working days, two dominant models have emerged from this evolution: remote work and hybrid work.

Remote Work Model

Remote work refers to performing work by employees from a location outside the traditional office environment. This model offers various advantages:

a. Flexibility: Employees can work from anywhere, allowing them to balance personal and professional responsibilities more effectively.

b. Cost Savings: Both employers and employees can save on costs related to office space, commuting, and other overheads.

c. Increased Productivity: Many studies suggest that remote workers can be more productive due to fewer office distractions and the ability to create a personalized work environment.

d. Access to a Global Talent Pool: Employers are not limited by geographic constraints, enabling them to hire the best talent from around the world.

However, the remote work also presents challenges:

a. Isolation: Employees may feel disconnected from their team colleagues, which can have a psychological impact on them, resulting in lower morale and teamwork.

b. Communication Issues: Internet bandwidth and connectivity are critical for remote work, and many times, it becomes an issue leading to misunderstandings or a lack of clarity.

c. Management Difficulties: Managers may find it challenging to supervise and evaluate remote employees effectively. The commitment of certain employees can be a challenge.

Hybrid Work Model

Hybrid work combines elements of both remote and in-office work. Employees can decide within their project teams which days to come to the Office, while the Organization would expect 2 to 3 days of presence in the office at minimum. This model aims to offer the best of both worlds:

a. Balanced Flexibility and Structure: Employees get the flexibility of remote work, while still having opportunities for in-office collaboration and engagement with the teams.

b. Enhanced Collaboration: Regular in-office days facilitate team meetings, brainstorming sessions, and social interactions, which are crucial for fostering innovation and team cohesion.

c. Improved Work-Life Balance: Employees can manage their responsibilities, while also benefiting from the support and resources available in the office.

Challenges of the hybrid model include:

a. Coordination Complexity: Scheduling and coordinating between remote and in-office days can be logistically challenging.

b. Technology Requirements: Effective hybrid work requires robust technology solutions to support seamless communication and collaboration.

Preferred Model in Today's IT world

The preferred work model today largely depends on the nature of the business, job roles, and individual preferences. However, there are some prevailing trends:

a. Hybrid Model as Preference: Many organizations are adopting hybrid models as the new standard, offering a balance that caters to diverse employee needs and business requirements. It allows companies to retain the flexibility and cost benefits of remote work while maintaining the advantages of in-person collaboration.

b. Industry-Specific Preferences: Certain industries, such as technology and creative fields, are more inclined towards remote and hybrid models due to the nature of their work. In contrast, sectors like manufacturing and healthcare may require more in-person presence.

c. Employee Preference: Considerable employees now expect at least partial remote work as part of their job. Some Organizations have started defining Job roles with Remote work as an option. The companies that offer flexible work arrangements are often more attractive to top talent.

d. Evolving Technology: Evolution in collaboration tools, project management software, and virtual reality are making remote and hybrid work more viable and efficient.

Conclusion

The rise of remote and hybrid work models signifies a fundamental shift in how the industry approaches work. While remote work provides unmatched flexibility, many organizations now prefer the hybrid model, which balances flexibility with the need for in-office interaction. As technology continues to evolve and cultural attitudes shift across different regions, it is likely that these work models will adapt further, shaping the future of work for IT professionals and others in various fields.

Increasing Demand for Cybersecurity Experts

In today's digital landscape, cybersecurity poses a significant challenge for businesses, governments, and individuals alike. With the rise of diverse and sophisticated cyber threats, the complexity and frequency of incidents have grown considerably. Consequently, the demand for cybersecurity experts has surged. This section examines the reasons for this increasing need and explores future trends in the field of cybersecurity.

Factors Driving the Demand for Cybersecurity Experts

We will consider the various factors that are enabling the requirements for cyber security professionals.

a. Rise in Cyber Threats: Over time, the varied occurrence and sophistication of cyberattacks have grown exponentially. As the technology grows, so are the ways of cyber threats. Cybercriminals utilize advanced tactics such as ransomware, phishing, and distributed denial-of-service (DDoS) attacks, targeting vulnerabilities in systems and networks. Highly skilled cybersecurity professionals are required to protect, detect, and mitigate against these threats proactively.

b. Digital Revolution: Organizations across all sectors are embracing digital transformation to enhance efficiency, and innovation to remain competitive. This shift involves the adoption of cloud computing, Gen AI and big data analytics. While these technologies offer high benefits, they also give rise to new security challenges, increasing the need for cybersecurity expertise.

c. Regulatory Compliance: The Governments in various Countries and worldwide regulatory bodies are directing stringent data protection laws and cybersecurity regulations, to protect the common users. Compliance with regulations such as the General Data Protection Regulation (GDPR), the Health Insurance Portability and Accountability Act (HIPAA), and the California Consumer Privacy Act (CCPA) requires organizations to have robust cybersecurity measures in place. Providing proactive mitigation of risks and vulnerabilities drives the demand for experts who can ensure compliance.

d. Work Environments: The rise of remote and hybrid work models has increased the attack opportunities for cybercriminals. Securing remote work environments, including home networks and personal devices, has become a vital need. Cybersecurity experts are required to develop and enforce security policies, implement secure authentication and access controls, and provide meticulous tracking.

e. High Impact Cyber Incidents: High-profile cyber incidents, such as the SolarWinds attack and the Colonial Pipeline ransomware attack, have heightened awareness of cybersecurity risks. These incidents highlight the potential impact of cyber threats on national security, critical infrastructure, and business continuity, inducing nations and organizations to invest more in cybersecurity.

Future Trends in Cybersecurity

We will now look at the future trends with the latest upcoming technologies within cyber security.

a. Artificial Intelligence and Machine Learning: AI and machine learning are revolutionizing cybersecurity by enhancing proactive threat detection, response, and prevention capabilities. These technologies can synthesize enormous data to identify patterns and anomalies, enabling swift and accurate identification of potential threats. Cybersecurity experts are bound to leverage AI to develop advanced defensive tools and techniques. There is a lot of scope for Innovation.

b. Zero Trust Architecture: The traditional perimeter-based security model is becoming outdated, as organizations adopt the Zero Trust approach. The traditional model was designed with an implicit level of trust. Unfortunately, cloud hosting, remote work, and other modernization make it difficult to rely on. These challenges can be addressed by implementing Zero Trust architecture, wherein all traffic moving into, out of, or within a corporate network is very well verified, inspected, and logged.

c. Cybersecurity for IoT and 5G: The high growth of IoT devices and the rollout of 5G networks present new security challenges. The IoT devices often lack robust security features, making them easy targets for attackers. The 5G networks, with their high speed and low latency, will facilitate new applications but will introduce more vulnerabilities. The cybersecurity experts will be required to develop strong solutions to secure these upcoming technologies.

d. Quantum Computing: Quantum computing has the high capability to break current security methods with encryption, posing a significant threat to data security. As quantum technology advances, cybersecurity experts will be required to develop quantum-resistant encryption algorithms to safeguard systems and sensitive information.

e. Cyber Resilience: Organizations are shifting their focus from mere prevention to cyber resilience—the ability to proactively prepare for, respond to, and recover from cyber incidents. This holistic approach includes robust incident response plans, regular security training, and continuous monitoring. Cybersecurity professionals will have a crucial role in building and maintaining cyber resilience.

f. Human-Oriented Security: Recognizing that humans are often the weakest link in cybersecurity. There is expected to be increased emphasis on user education and awareness. The cybersecurity experts will work on designing user-friendly security solutions and conducting regular awareness training to ensure that users understand and follow best practices, and do not get distracted by the vulnerability-oriented communications.

g. Shortage of Skilled People: Considering highly growing demands, there is a significant shortage of skilled cybersecurity professionals. This gap is expected to increase, leading the organizations to invest in upskilling and reskill of the people, with training programs, partnerships with educational institutions, and initiatives to attract and retain talent.

Conclusion

The growing demand for cybersecurity experts is driven by the evolving threats associated with digital transformation, regulatory requirements, and shifts in work environments. As cybersecurity continues to advance, future trends such as artificial intelligence (AI), Zero Trust architecture, Internet of Things (IoT) and 5G security, quantum computing, cyber resilience, human-centric security, and the persistent skills shortage will create new professional opportunities. IT professionals with cybersecurity expertise will be essential in safeguarding our digital lives.

The Impact of Digital Transformation on IT Roles

Digital transformation refers to the integration of digital technology across all aspects of a business, fundamentally changing how organizations operate and deliver value to their clients and end users. This transformative process significantly affects IT roles, redefining their responsibilities, skill requirements, and career paths. In this discussion, we will explore the impact of digital transformation on IT roles.

Evolution of IT Roles

With the digital transformation, new IT roles are evolving. We shall refer to how these reflect on the skills requirements and in turn the career path for individuals.

a. Transition from Maintenance to Innovation:

- Traditional IT Roles: Historically, IT roles were primarily focused on maintenance and support of legacy systems, ensuring systems and infrastructure are up and running.

- IT Roles with Transformation: With digital transformation, there is a paradigm shift towards innovation and strategic initiatives. The IT professionals are now expected to derive business growth by leveraging technology, creating innovative products, and services, and smoothing the customer experiences.

b. Evolution of New Specializations:

- Data Science and Analytics: As organizations increasingly rely on data-driven decision-making, the demand for data scientists, data analysts, and business intelligence experts is rapidly increasing. These roles aim to extract insights from data to advise crucial business strategies.

- Cybersecurity: With the rise of digital threats, cybersecurity has become a critical area. Cybersecurity specialists, ethical hackers, and information security analysts are instrumental in protecting organizational digital assets.

- Cloud Computing: The transition from legacy to cloud-based solutions has become essential to all businesses, to keep the cost under control. This has created a need for cloud architects, engineers, and security experts, who can design, implement, and manage cloud environments and applications.

- DevOps and Automation: The DevOps practices adopted by the organizations minimize the delivery turn-around time. The roles such as DevOps engineers and automation specialists, stress aligning development, testing and deployment processes and achieving integration with continuous delivery.

c. Integration of Business and IT:

- Business Analysts: These professionals are the bridge between IT and business units, ensuring that technological solutions align with business goals.

- Product Managers: The product managers serve as a fulcrum with a strong understanding of business requirements, coordinating business users and technology teams. They are responsible for the success of digital products required by the business.

- Digital Transformation Leaders: This role oversees the overall digital transformation strategy, ensuring that technology initiatives support the organization's vision.

Changing Skill Requirements

With the new upcoming roles, the skills requirements as well changing in line with it.

We would see how it would reflect on the technical, soft skills and Leadership skills.

a. Technical Skills:

- Latest Technologies: IT professionals need to be proficient in emerging technologies such as artificial intelligence, machine learning, blockchain, and the Internet of Things (IoT). IT professionals need to be adaptable and open to continuous learning for the rapidly changing technology.

- Cloud Computing: The skills in cloud platforms like AWS, Azure, Google, and IBM Cloud are essential as organizations migrate their legacy infrastructure and services to the cloud.

- Cybersecurity: Knowledge and skills of security protocols, threat detection, and mitigation strategies are critical to protect against rising cyber threats.

b. Soft Skills:

- Communication: While interacting with Management and Clients, the right communication becomes very vital.

- Collaboration: As IT becomes the core of most business units, interpersonal skills, collaboration, and teamwork get prominence.

- Problem-Solving: The complex challenges in Digital transformation require innovative abilities to solve any issue and achieve customer satisfaction.

c. Leadership with Strategic Thinking:

- Strategic Vision: IT leaders should wear the Client's shoes and drive digital initiatives that align with organizational goals.

- Strong Leadership: IT professionals require effective communication and interpersonal skills to move into a leadership role. Good communication skill helps leaders explain complex tech concepts and build relationships with their colleagues and clients.

- Risk-taking: The IT Managers and Leaders need to take calculated risks to increase and execute the business. The skill requires maturity and experience.

Impact on Career Paths

The transformation will have an immense impact on the individual's skills and relevant career paths. And the opportunities could grow rapidly.

a. Loads of Opportunities:

- Career Diversification: Digital transformation offers IT professionals various opportunities to diversify their careers by moving into high-demand roles such as data science, cybersecurity, or cloud computing.

- Leadership Roles: With a technology-driven business strategy, there are more opportunities for IT professionals to move into leadership positions, such as Chief Information Officer (CIO), Chief Technology Officer (CTO) or Chief Data Officer (CDO).

b. Continuous Learning:

- Professional skills: IT professionals must have continuous learning to keep up with evolving technologies and methodologies. The Certifications, badges, advanced studies, and online courses are valuable for skills development and career advancement.

- Cross-Domain Skills: Gaining skills that span multiple domains and technology platforms, such as business acumen combined with technical expertise, can enhance career prospects.

Conclusion

The digital transformation is rehauling the landscape of IT roles, shifting the focus from maintenance and support to innovation, creating new opportunities and specializations. IT professionals must acquire new technical skills, enhance soft skills, develop leadership skills, adopting continuous learning. As IT becomes the core of business strategy, the business and IT roles will continue to deepen integration. This will provide expanded career opportunities and the potential for IT professionals to play a pivotal role in driving organizational and client success.

The Shift Towards Agile and DevOps Practices

In the rapidly evolving landscape of IT, Agile and DevOps practices have emerged as crucial methodologies, revolutionizing how organizations work to develop, deploy, and manage hardware and software. This transition is driven by the need for greater flexibility, and faster delivery, to deliver more reliable systems. We will have a comprehensive look at how Agile and DevOps practices are transforming IT roles and workflows.

Understanding Agile and DevOps

Agile and DevOps have become proven ways of working, enhancing the quality of work, turnaround time, and time to market. It has been established as defined strategic methodologies, which have become industry standard.

Agile Methodology

- Principles: The Agile methodology is a project management approach that involves breaking the project into smaller iterations and emphasizes continuous collaboration and improvement. The teams follow iterations of planning, executing, and evaluating. It emphasizes flexibility, continuous improvement, and customer feedback.

- Frameworks: Common Agile frameworks include Scrum/Iteration, Kanban, Lean, and Extreme Programming (XP), each with its defined practices and focus areas.

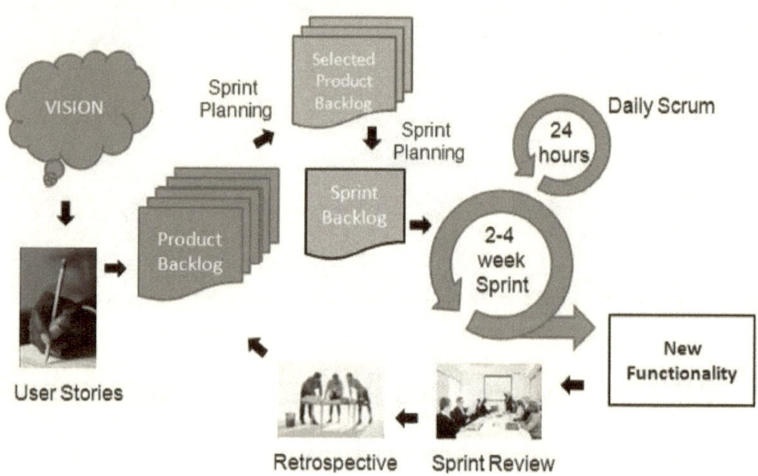

With a defined vision, certain user stories are consolidated by the Product Owner as the Product backlog. With Sprint planning, the product backlog is prioritized and split into small manageable Sprints. With the Sprint or Iteration cycle, the agile teams produce the most valued product features. The Sprint review takes place with the stakeholders providing immediate feedback. A Retrospective takes place to review the lessons learned. This Agile cycle iterates for the multiple sprints until the product backlog is solutioned adequately.

Success story of Spotify with Scaling Agile

Spotify, the popular music streaming service, faced challenges for rapid growth and was required to scale its development improving its agility and innovation. As they expanded their operations, the legacy delivery model faced severe constraints, hampering the time to market.

Spotify adopted a Scaling Agile model based on Tribes, Squads, Chapters, and Guilds. Squads are small teams with 5 to 10 people, who have all skills required for a module, for which they are responsible. Tribes are groups of Squads working on related sub-domain areas. Chapters ensure technical excellence across Squads (like DBAs), and Guilds are communities of common interest.

With this Agile model transformation, Spotify achieved a high level of agility with scaling. Being fully responsible, Squads were autonomous, leading to faster development cycles, increased innovation, and enhanced product quality.

DevOps Practices

- Principles: DevOps combines software development (Dev) and IT operations (Ops) to optimize the overall delivery lifecycle while delivering features, fixes, and updates, more frequently in close alignment with the client's business objectives.

- Key Practices: Continuous integration (CI), continuous delivery/ deployment (CD), infrastructure as code (IaC), automated testing, and monitoring.

DevOps aggregates the literary ideas, practices, and tools that increase an organization's ability to deliver applications and services at high velocity.

Using DevOps principles, organizations can evolve and improve products faster than organizations that use traditional software development and infrastructure management processes. Adopting DevOps optimizes the turn-around time and enables organizations to serve their customers faster and compete more effectively.

Success Story of Google with DevOps

We would refer to the story of Google, for implementing the DevOps as strategy. Google is a torchbearer in the technological Innovation. Google implemented automation and continuous delivery, focusing on innovation and collaboration. They used Site Reliability Engineering to maintain their service reliability.

Some examples of how Google has implemented DevOps include:

- **Infrastructure as Code (IaC):** Google implemented Infrastructure as Code (IaC) tools like Terraform to manage their infrastructure. This helped to automate the deployment and configuration of the applications and infrastructure, reducing manual errors and improving reliability.

- **Continuous delivery:** Google converged their continuous delivery. They implemented automated testing, progressive rollout, and other DevOps practices to enable continuous delivery at scale.

These DevOps practices have helped Google to achieve remarkable results. By incorporating DevOps practices, Google has built and maintained one of the world's most innovative and reliable services.

Impact on IT Roles

As the IT roles are evolving, the Agile and DevOps methodologies have an impact on it, on the way of working. With the adoption of these, the way of working has become more mature and sophisticated, giving faster qualitative results.

a. Enhanced Collaboration:

- Cross-Functional Teams: Agile and DevOps streamline communication between development, operations, and other IT functions, fostering a culture of collaboration and shared responsibility.

- Communication Skills: IT professionals require strong communication and teamwork skills to work effectively in integrated teams.

b. Shift in Responsibilities:

- From Specialized to T-shaped Skills: IT professionals are encouraged to develop T-shaped skills, where they have deep expertise in one technology area and a broad understanding of other areas. This enables greater flexibility and collaboration within teams.

- End-to-end Ownership: In DevOps, teams (called squads) take end-to-end responsibility for the applications they develop from getting requirements, and writing code to deployment and maintenance, ensuring higher accountability and quality.

c. New Roles and Specializations:

- DevOps Engineers: These professionals bridge the gap between development and operations, focusing on automating and streamlining the software delivery process.

- Site Reliability Engineers (SREs): The SREs apply software engineering principles to system administration tasks, focusing on reliability and scalability.

- Agile Coaches: They help teams adopt Agile practices, facilitating training, mentoring, and process improvements.

Benefits of Agile and DevOps Practices

The practices with Agile and DevOps have nurtured the project delivery for betterment. We shall see the benefits of following these practices.

a. Improved Efficiency and Productivity:

- Reduced Turn-around time: The Agile and DevOps practices reduce the time required to develop, test, and deploy new features, enhancing productivity, and reducing the time to market.

- Automation: Automating repetitive tasks frees up IT professional's time to focus on higher-value activities and innovation.

b. Higher Quality and Reliability:

- Automated Testing: Continuous testing ensures that code changes do not introduce new defects, delivering more stable and reliable software.

- Proactive Issue Resolution: Continuous monitoring helps detect and resolve issues before they reach Production environments, affecting end users.

c. Greater Flexibility and Responsiveness:

- Adaptability: Agile practices enable teams to respond quickly to changing requirements and market conditions, ensuring that the product stays relevant and competitive.

- Customer-Centric Development: Frequent releases and feedback from clients ensure that the product meets customer requirements and expectations.

Conclusion

> Adopting Agile and DevOps practices aligns with a fundamental change in how IT professionals deliver software and operations. By fostering collaboration, automating workflows, and emphasizing continuous improvement, these methodologies help organizations deliver higher-quality software faster and more reliable manner. For IT professionals, embracing Agile and DevOps leads to acquiring new skills, adopting new roles, and continuously learning to stay ahead in a dynamic and fast-paced environment. This transformation empowers IT professionals to drive innovation and deliver greater value to their organizations and customers.

Growing Importance of Data-Driven Decision Making

In the current business scenario, data has become a critical asset, for making strategic decisions, affecting the future of organizations. Data-driven decision-making (DDDM) is the process of using data to inform your decision-making process and validate a course of action before executing it. It refers to the approach of making decisions on data analysis and interpretation, rather than intuition or observation alone. It involves using data analytics and methodologies to lead business strategies and operational decisions. For IT professionals, this model shift has deep implications, with way of working, transforming roles, responsibilities, and skill requirements.

Nandan Nilkeni, Co-founder of Infosys and Chairman of UIDAI said "Data has become the new oil. Just like oil was the basis for the transformation of the 20th century, data is the basis for the 21st century."

We will explore the growing importance of DDDM and its impact, along with the benefits to IT professionals.

Importance of DDDM

a. Accuracy and Objectivity:

- Based on real-time data, Organizations can make more accurate and objective decisions, reducing the influence of bias and assumptions.

- Data analytics enables better forecasting and trend analysis, allowing organizations to forecast market trends and align strategy proactively.

b. Efficiency and Performance:

- The Data insights can pinpoint inefficiencies and areas for performance improvement, resulting in optimized operations and cost savings.

- The Organizations can track and measure performance metrics more diligently, driving continuous improvement.

c. Competitive Advantage:

- The Data analysis offers real-time insights into market trends, user behaviour, and competitive dynamics, helping organizations to be proactive and remain ahead of the competition.

- The Data-driven insights can explore new opportunities for innovation and growth, promoting a culture of innovation.

d. Personalization and Customer Experience:

- Understanding customer preferences and behaviour through data enables personalized marketing, improved customer service, and enhanced overall customer experience.

- Product Development: Data-driven feedback and usage analytics can be input to product development and feature enhancements, ensuring products meet customer expectations.

Impact on IT Roles

a. Emergence of New Roles:

- Data Scientists: Specialists who analyse and interpret complex data sets to extract actionable insights. They use statistical methods, machine learning, and data visualization tools.

- Data Engineers: Professionals who design, build, and maintain the infrastructure for data generation, collection, and storage. They ensure data is accessible and reliable for analysis.

- Business Intelligence Analysts: Experts who use data visualization and reporting tools to help businesses understand their data and make informed decisions.

b. Skill Development:

- Analytical Skills: IT professionals need strong analytical skills to interpret data and derive meaningful insights.

- Proficiency in Tools and Technologies: Familiarity with data analysis tools (such as Python, R, SQL), data visualization software (such as Tableau, and Power BI), and big data technologies (such as Hadoop, and Spark) is necessary.

- Understanding of Machine Learning and AI: Knowledge of machine learning algorithms and artificial intelligence is increasingly important for advanced data analysis and predictive modelling.

c. Collaborative Approach:

- Cross-functional collaboration: IT professionals must work closely with business stakeholders, sales and marketing teams, and other departments to understand their data needs and provide relevant analysis and insights.

- Communication Skills: The ability to communicate complex data findings in a clear and actionable manner is crucial for driving data-driven decision-making.

Benefits of DDDM for IT Professionals

a. Strategic Influence:

- Increased Role in Strategy: IT professionals are increasingly involved in strategic planning and decision-making processes, leveraging their data expertise to guide business direction.

- Leadership Opportunities: Expertise in data analytics opens leadership opportunities, such as Chief Data Officer (CDO) or other executive roles focused on data strategy.

b. Career Growth:

- High Demand for Skills: The demand for data-savvy IT professionals continues to grow, offering various career opportunities and competitive salaries.

- Continuous Learning: The fast-evolving field of data analytics encourages continuous learning and professional development, keeping IT professionals engaged and up to date with the latest trends.

c. Enhanced Job Satisfaction:

- Impactful Work: Working on data-driven projects that directly influence business outcomes can be highly rewarding and satisfying.

- Problem-Solving: The analytical and problem-solving nature of data-driven roles provides intellectual stimulation and challenges.

Success Story of Uber with DDDM

Uber's success with its data-driven strategy is an inspiring story. Uber exclusively uses data to improve their pricing in real-time. The app leverages real-time data and tracks insights like User behaviour (essentially during rush hours), current traffic situations, weather scenarios (Rain, snow, etc.) and public transportation availability and accessibility.

Based on these factors, the Uber application modifies the prices and shows the most favourable rates for users at any required time. Machine learning helps to predict when and where the demand can be high. It uses a mix of historical and current data from the application, which further helps Uber to align supply with demand effectively.

Conclusion

The data-driven decisions are driving critical aspects of modern organizations. The power of data lies in its ability to provide objective insights, improve accuracy, and enhance decision-making processes. By exploring the data, organizations can have an in-depth understanding of the customers, streamline operations, and work out effective strategies. The growing importance of data-driven decision-making is reshaping the landscape for IT professionals.

As organisations increasingly rely on data to drive their strategies and operations, the demand for skilled data professionals continues to rise. IT roles are evolving to include new specialisations, requiring a good combination of technical, analytical, and communication skills. Adopting DDDM enhances business performance and competitiveness and offers IT professionals new career opportunities and the potential for significant impact within their organisations.

Chapter 3

Important IT Roles and Career Paths

The IT industry is growing robustly. It has entered deep into all the commercial industries and everyday life of individuals. It has developed certain structured roles and career paths. We will explore the key IT roles and the career opportunities in it.

Traditional IT Roles vs. Emerging IT Roles

Information Technology (IT) offers a diverse range of roles and career paths, catering to the aspirations and skills of individuals. As technology continues to evolve, the opportunities within IT expand as well. We will oversee key IT roles and potential career paths for IT professionals, depicting the skills and expertise required for each.

Core IT Roles

The Core IT roles remain at the heart of the organisations. As the industry has evolved over the years, these roles have matured in the IT company's defined role/responsibility structure.

a. Application Developer:

- Responsibilities: Develop an application which satisfies the requirements of the client. For this purpose, carry out low-level design, develop, test, and maintain software applications and systems. This role involves development/coding, unit testing, deployment, UAT support, and Defect fixes.

- Skills Required: Programming languages (e.g., Java, Angular, Node.js, Python, C++), problem-solving abilities, understanding of software development methodologies (Agile, DevOps), version control systems (e.g., GitHub), Integrated Development Environment (IDE – Eclipse, RAD).

b. Test Specialist:

- Responsibilities: Ensure software quality, improve user experience, and help identify risks by rigorously testing software applications. For this to achieve, create and update test cases and test scripts, test APIs, QA, and user acceptance testing, prepare test data and execute test transactions, Integration and Regression Testing.

- Skills Required: Analytical skills, working in an agile methodology and troubleshooting problems, effective communication skills, manual testing, and exposure to automation.

c. Business Analyst:

- Responsibilities: Analyse information systems to meet client needs. This includes gathering requirements, creating business system specifications, and coordinating with developers and stakeholders.

- Skills Required: Analytical thinking, understanding of business processes, strong communication skills esp writing skills, and knowledge of system design and analysis tools.

d. Network Administrator:

- Responsibilities: Support and maintain client's computer networks, ensuring reliable network performance and security. The job work includes configuring network hardware, troubleshooting issues, and monitoring network activities.

- Skills Required: Knowledge of network protocols and services (TCP/IP, DNS, DHCP), experience with network hardware (routers, switches), and understanding of network security principles.

e. Database Administrator (DBA):

- Responsibilities: Support and maintain databases to ensure their performance, security, and availability. This includes database design, backup and recovery, and performance tuning.

- Skills Required: Specialized skills in database management systems (e.g., MySQL, Oracle, DB2, SQL Server), understanding of SQL, data modelling, and adequate problem-solving skills.

f. Cybersecurity Specialist:

- Responsibilities: Protect an organization's information systems from cyber threats. The job work includes implementing proactive security measures, monitoring for security breaches, and responding to security incidents.

- Skills Required: Knowledge of cybersecurity principles, familiarity with security tools (firewalls, intrusion detection systems), understanding of encryption and authentication methods, and analytical skills.

g. Application Architect:

- Responsibilities: Architecture of the application based on client needs, High-Level design, Strategy for technology and identification of suitable tech stack, and Application Performance in Production.

- Skills Required: Solution Requirements documentation, Solution Architecture, High-level and Low-level Design, In-depth knowhow of Legacy and Emerging technologies in the market, and Design Patterns.

h. Cloud Architect:

- Responsibilities: Design and manage an organization's cloud computing strategy - cloud migration plans, application design, and cloud environment management and monitoring.

- Skills Required: Knowledge of cloud platforms (AWS, Azure, Google, IBM Cloud), experience with cloud services and infrastructure, and understanding of network and security fundamentals.

i. IT Project Manager:

- Responsibilities: Plan, execute, and oversee IT projects to ensure they are planned and tracked well, for completion on time and within budget, and delivered adhering to quality norms. This includes coordinating with the team, managing resources, and communicating with stakeholders, reporting to management.

- Skills Required: Project management methodologies (e.g., Agile, Waterfall), leadership, negotiation, risk management, and strong communication abilities.

j. Further to IT Project Manager, there are Leadership and Management roles like Program Manager, Portfolio Manager, Account Manager, Practice Leader, Industry Leader, Service Line Leader, Sector Leader, CIC Leader among others.

Emerging IT Roles

As the IT Industry is evolving with new technologies, new roles and responsibilities are evolving. We shall see the emerging IT roles, with the skills needed for the new technology environment.

a. Data Scientist:

- Responsibilities: Analyse large sets of data to extract meaningful insights and support decision-making processes. This involves using statistical methods, machine learning, and data visualization.

- Skills Required: Proficiency in programming languages (Python, R), understanding of statistical and machine learning algorithms, data synthesis, and data visualization tools (e.g., Cognos TM1, Tableau, Power BI).

b. DevOps Engineer:

- Responsibilities: Fulcrum between software development and IT operations by automating and streamlining the development and deployment processes. This includes managing Cloud environment CI/CD pipelines, infrastructure as code, and monitoring.

- Skills Required: Knowledge of DevOps tools (Jenkins, Docker, Kubernetes), scripting languages (Bash, Python), various cloud platforms, and cloud environment support.

c. AI/Machine Learning Engineer:

- Responsibilities: Develop and deploy AI and machine learning models to solve complex problems and improve business processes. This includes data preprocessing, model training, and implementation.

- Skills Required: Proficiency in machine learning frameworks (TensorFlow, PyTorch), programming skills (Python, Java), understanding of algorithms and data structures, and experience with data science tools.

d. Blockchain Developer:

- Responsibilities: Design and develop blockchain applications and smart contracts. This includes understanding blockchain architecture, developing decentralized applications (dApps), and ensuring security.

- Skills Required: Knowledge of blockchain platforms (Ethereum, Hyperledger), proficiency in smart contract languages (Solidity), understanding of cryptographic principles, and familiarity with decentralized technologies.

e. Internet of Things (IoT) Specialist:

- Responsibilities: Develop and manage IoT solutions, including device connectivity, data collection, and integration with other systems. This involves working with sensors, networks, and IoT platforms.

- Skills Required: Knowledge of IoT protocols (MQTT, CoAP), experience with IoT platforms (AWS, Azure - IoT Hubs), understanding of embedded systems, and data analytics.

f. Process Automation Engineer:

- Responsibilities: Define current process flow, determine process steps/stages, identify stage inputs and outputs, create routine decisions, implement process definitions into process automation tools, and deploy the automated process.

- Skills Required: Scripting, programming, ability to use automation tools, analytical skills, data analysis. The UiPath Business Automation Platform, the SS&C Blue Prism product portfolio, IBM Robotic Process Automation, and Appian RPA are some of the best tools in the market at present.

The Robotic Process Automation (RPA) is coming up very fast. It streamlines workflows and makes it easy to build, deploy, and manage software robots that emulate humans' actions interacting with digital systems and software. It optimizes the human interaction and achieves high efficiency and cost savings.

Career Paths in IT

It is important to refer to the wider canvas of the IT industry, with various career paths for individuals. Keeping an eye on these paths, you can take calculated steps to move progressively in your career.

➤ Technical Specialist Path

- Progression in Development Stream:

  The career for the Application Developer starts as a Graduate hire with development testing. With further career growth, the professional can reach various management and leadership roles, up to the CTO level of a company. It is depicted in the diagram below. There are various technical languages, that the developer can learn and adopt for implementation of client requirements.

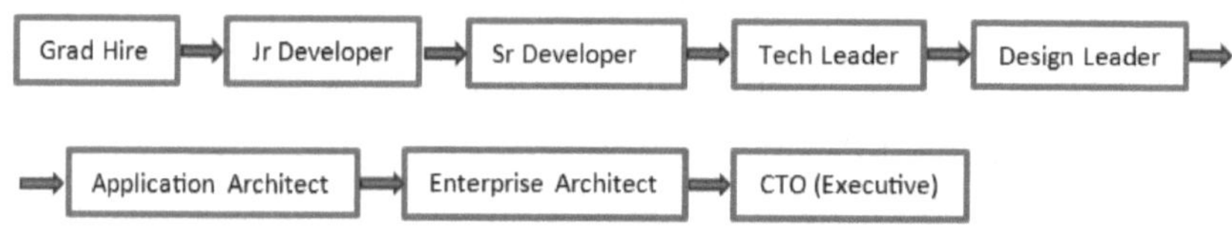

- Progression in Testing Stream:

  There are 2 streams in Testing. viz Manual Testing, Test Automation. Manual Testing is traditional testing, in which the Test Specialist creates the Test cases based on the business requirements. He then carries out manual testing of the application and generates the test results.

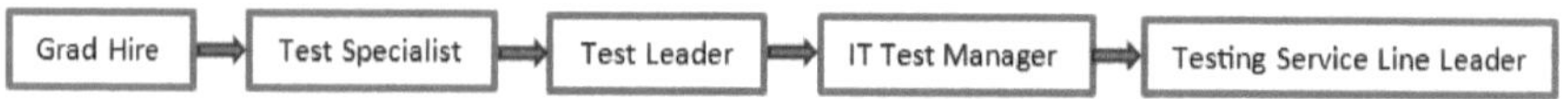

  Test Automation is another promising area. It further requires skills to be acquired in various Automation Tools usage. There are various tools in the market like Selenium, Appium (mobile testing), LambdaTest (testing on cloud), Tricentis Tosca, and Apache JMeter, among others. Some basic Java or scripting knowledge helps so that the Automation scripts can be written fluently.

  While individuals are inclined to become an application developer, the Test Specialist career path is equally important. With recent technology growth, Test Automation and Process Automation provide career growth opportunities for testing professionals.

- Focus: Deepening technical expertise and taking on complex technical challenges. This path involves staying current with technological advancements and continuously improving technical skills.

➤ Management Path

- Progression: The PM career progression can follow the below path.

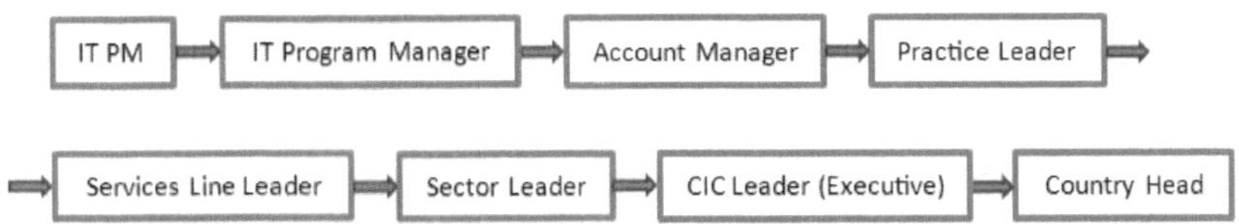

- Focus: Overseeing IT operations, managing teams, and aligning IT strategy with business goals. This path requires strong leadership, communication, project management, strategic planning and risk-taking skills.

The Organizations with a Matrix structure have a People manager as an add-on responsibility, further to the PM role, which includes addressing the people's career aspirations, and growth along with rewards, salary etc people-oriented matters.

➤ Hybrid Path

- Progression: The career change from Application development to a DevOps role will appear as a Hybrid career path. It will look as below.

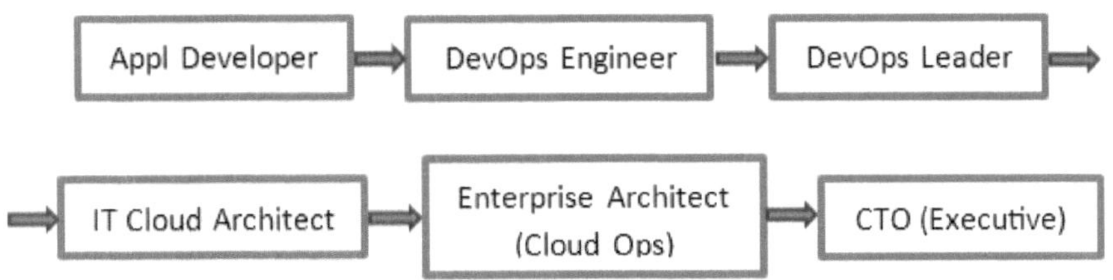

- Focus: Combining technical skills with operational expertise to manage and optimize IT infrastructure and processes. This path emphasises both technical proficiency and managerial capabilities.

Conclusion

The IT field presents a variety of roles and career paths, each with its own risks and rewards. As business and technology advance, new opportunities will continue to arise, necessitating that IT professionals adapt and broaden their skill sets. Whether one chooses to specialize in a technical area, transition into management, or pursue a hybrid role, IT professionals can find rewarding careers that align with their goals and abilities.

Career Paths in Software Development

Software development is a dynamic and multi-faceted field offering various career opportunities and paths. Among the most prominent paths are front-end development, back-end development, and full-stack development. Each of these requires distinct skill sets and offers unique career opportunities to start with. We will oversee these career paths:

Front-End Development

Overview

The Front-end developers are responsible for the client side of web applications. They focus on the visual aspects and user interactions, ensuring that applications are user-friendly, responsive, intuitive, and aesthetically pleasing.

➤ Key Responsibilities

- Designing and implementing the user interface (UI).

- Ensuring cross-browser compatibility and responsive design.

- Optimizing web applications for speed and performance.

- Collaborating with designers to create a seamless user experience.

- Maintaining and improving the user-interfacing features of the application.

➤ Skills Required

- Languages: HTML, CSS, JavaScript.

- Frameworks/Libraries: React, Angular, Vue.js.

- Tools: Version control (GitHub), package managers (npm, Yarn), build tools (Webpack, Gulp).

- Design Principles: Understanding of UX/UI design principles, accessibility standards, and responsive design.

- Soft Skills: Creativity, attention to detail, communication skills.

➤ Career Progression

1. Junior Front-End Developer: Entry-level role focused on learning and implementing basic UI elements under supervision.

2. Senior Front-End Developer: More responsibility in designing and developing complex UI components, participating in code reviews, and collaborating closely with designers.

3. Front-End Technical Lead: Leading front-end projects, mentoring junior developers, and making architectural decisions.

4. Front-End Architect: Overseeing the overall architecture of the front-end stack, ensuring scalability and performance, and setting development standards.

Back-End Development

Overview

The Back-end developers focus on the server side of web applications. They develop the logic, database interactions, authentication, server configuration, and API integration that power the front-end interfaces.

➤ Key Responsibilities

- Developing server-side logic and managing database connections.

- Creating and maintaining APIs for front-end consumption.

- Ensuring data security and integrity.

- Implementing authentication and authorization systems.

- Fine-tune server performance and scalability to optimize user response time

➤ Skills Required

- Languages: Java, Python, Ruby, PHP, Node.js.

- Frameworks: Express.js, Django, Spring, Ruby on Rails.

- Databases: SQL (MySQL, PostgreSQL) and NoSQL (MongoDB, Cassandra).

- Tools: Version control (GitHub), containerization (Docker), continuous integration (Jenkins, CircleCI).

- Concepts: Understanding of RESTful services, microservices architecture, and security practices.

- Soft Skills: Problem-solving, logical thinking, attention to detail.

➤ Career Progression

1. Junior Back-End Developer: Focused on writing server-side code and learning database management under guidance.

2. Senior Back-End Developer: Taking on more complex server-side tasks, database design, and API development.

3. Back-End Technical Lead: Leading back-end projects, optimizing server performance, and mentoring junior developers.

4. Back-End Architect: Designing the overall architecture of the server-side infrastructure, ensuring scalability, security, and performance.

Full-Stack Development

Overview

The Full-stack developers are versatile professionals skilled in both front-end and back-end development. They have a comprehensive understanding of how web applications function from end to end, making them valuable assets for development teams. This is the latest trend of career for developers to start with. It requires training and implementation experience in both front-end and back-end technologies and processes.

➤ Key Responsibilities

- Developing and maintaining both client-side and server-side components.

- Ensuring seamless integration between the front-end and back-end.

- Managing databases and server infrastructure.

- Collaborating with other developers, designers, and stakeholders.

- Troubleshooting and resolving issues across the entire stack.

➤ Skills Required

- Front-end: HTML, CSS, JavaScript, and frameworks like React or Angular.

- Back-End: Languages like Java, Python, Node.js, frameworks like Express.js or Django.

- Databases: SQL and NoSQL databases.

- Tools: Version control (GitHub), CI/CD tools, containerization (Docker).

- Concepts: Understanding of full-stack development principles, including MVC architecture, API development, and security best practices.

- Soft Skills: Adaptive, strong communication, problem-solving.

➤ Career Progression

1. Junior Full-Stack Developer: Learning and implementing basic features across both front-end and back-end under supervision.

2. Senior Full-Stack Developer: Handling more complex full-stack tasks, developing entire features independently.

3. Full-Stack Technical Lead: Leading full-stack projects, ensuring seamless integration, and mentoring junior developers.

4. Full-Stack Architect: Designing the overall architecture for full-stack applications, ensuring efficiency, scalability, performance and maintainability.

Conclusion

The career paths in software development are diverse and provide many opportunities for specialization and advancement. IT professionals can build rewarding careers by focusing on front-end, back-end, or full-stack development while continuously developing their skills, staying updated with technological advancements, and taking on increased responsibilities. Each path requires a unique set of skills and presents different challenges and rewards, allowing professionals to choose the one that best aligns with their aspirations and abilities.

Opportunities in IT Project Management

In IT project management, Agile methodologies and Scrum frameworks are becoming increasingly popular, and are continually evolving. These approaches emphasize flexibility, continuous improvement, and collaboration, offering IT professionals various opportunities for growth and leadership. We will explore the roles and opportunities within Agile Project Management and the specific responsibilities of a Scrum Master.

Agile Project Management

Overview

Agile project management is an iterative approach that focuses on delivering small, manageable defined parts of a project, known as iterations or sprints. This method allows teams to adapt to changes quickly, get client feedback iteratively and deliver value incrementally, improving product quality, and achieving higher customer satisfaction.

Key Principles of Agile

- Continuous Customer Collaboration: Involving customers throughout the development process to ensure their needs are met. The Design Thinking process could be used as a basis to start with the client, to know the personas along with business requirements.

- Response to Change: Adaptable and open to feedback, even late development cycle.

- Iterative Progress: Delivering work in small, manageable parts to allow for regular client reviews and updates.

- Empowered Teams: The teams have end-to-end responsibility for delivery. Encouraging self-organized teams to take ownership of their work and make decisions collectively.

Agile Roles and Responsibilities

a. Agile Project Manager

- Responsibilities: Oversee the Agile process, ensure the team adheres to Agile principles, facilitate communication between stakeholders, and remove obstacles that hinder progress.

- Skills Required: Strong understanding of Agile methodologies, excellent communication and leadership skills, ability to manage multiple Agile streams running in tandem, and proficiency in Agile tools (e.g., JIRA, Trello).

b. Product Owner

- Responsibilities: Define and prioritize the product backlog, represent the customer's interests, and ensure the team delivers value to the business. The PO is usually at the business team side role/responsibility, and interfaces with the business teams for requirements and funnels it to the delivery team with prioritization.

- Skills Required: Deep understanding of the product and market, strong communication skills, ability to prioritize tasks, and collaboration skills.

c. Development Team / Squad

- Responsibilities: Deliver incremental requirements of the product at the end of each sprint, participate in sprint planning, daily stand-ups, and retrospectives.

- Skills Required: Technical proficiency in relevant technologies, collaborative mindset, and problem-solving skills.

Scrum Master Role

Overview

The Scrum Master is a key role within the Scrum framework, one of the most popular Agile methodologies. The Scrum Master ensures that the Scrum team follows the Agile ceremonies, facilitating communication and collaboration both within the team and with external stakeholders.

➤ Key Responsibilities

- Facilitating Scrum Events: Organize and facilitate daily stand-ups, sprint planning, sprint reviews, and retrospectives.

- Removing Impediments: Identify and remove obstacles that hinder the team's progress and escalate any blockers to the Project Manager.

- Coaching the Team: Educate team members on Agile principles and practices, fostering a culture of continuous improvement.

- Promoting Collaboration: Encourage collaboration within the team and with external stakeholders, ensuring clear communication and transparency.

- Ensuring Adherence to Scrum Practices: Ensure that the team adheres to Agile ceremonies and maintains the integrity of the Scrum process.

➤ Skills Required

- In-depth knowledge of Scrum: Thorough understanding of Scrum principles, roles, events, and artefacts.

- Leadership and Facilitation: Strong leadership skills to guide the team and facilitate meetings effectively.

- Communication and Collaboration: Excellent communication skills to liaise between the team and stakeholders.

- Problem-solving: Ability to identify and resolve impediments that affect the team's progress.

- Coaching and Mentoring: Skills to educate and mentor team members on Agile practices and continuous improvement.

➤ Certifications for Career Progression

a. Certified Scrum Master (CSM): The certification that demonstrates knowledge of Scrum fundamentals and the role of a Scrum Master.

b. Certified Scrum Product Owner (CSPO): The certification deplores the business side processing requirements with prioritization, backlog management and collaboration with the development team.

c. Disciplined Agile Senior Scrum Master (PMI-DASSM): A higher-level certification for experienced Scrum Masters, focusing on advanced Scrum practices and leadership skills.

Opportunities in IT Project Management

a. Career Growth and Advancement:

- From Scrum Master to Agile Coach: Many Scrum-Masters advance to become Agile Coaches, who work with multiple teams and departments to implement Agile practices at a broader organizational level.

- Project Management Leadership: Experienced Agile project managers can move into senior leadership roles, such as Program Manager, Portfolio Manager, or Director.

b. Cross-Functional Experience:

- Diverse Project Involvement: Agile project managers often work on a variety of projects across different industries and domains, getting valuable experience and insights.

- Collaboration with Multiple Teams: The role involves working closely with development, QA, design, and business teams, providing an overall view of the project lifecycle.

c. High Demand for Skills:

- Growing Adoption of Agile: As more organizations adopt Agile methodologies, the demand for skilled Agile project managers and Scrum Masters continues to rise.

- Competitive Salaries: Due to their critical role in ensuring project success, Agile professionals often command competitive salaries and benefits.

d. Continuous Learning and Development:

- Emphasis on Improvement: Agile methodologies emphasize continuous improvement, providing opportunities for ongoing learning and professional development.

- Access to Training and Certification: Numerous training programs and certifications are available, helping professionals stay current and move ahead in the leadership ladder, with industry trends and best practices.

Conclusion

The field of IT project management, especially within Agile frameworks, presents numerous and diverse opportunities. Roles in Agile project management, such as Scrum Master, allow IT professionals to lead teams and enhance project success through continuous improvement. By gaining expertise in Agile methodologies and pursuing relevant training, badges, and certifications, IT professionals can advance their careers, assume leadership positions, and make significant contributions to their organizations' success.

Growing Field of Data Science and Analytics

The field of data science and analytics is rapidly growing, giving exciting career opportunities for IT professionals. Organizations are increasingly leveraging data to drive decision-making, refine operations, and gain competitive advantages. The key roles in this field include Data Engineers, Data Scientists, and Data Analysts. Each role has distinct responsibilities and requires specific skill sets. We shall see the key responsibilities, skills required and the progression path for these roles.

Data Engineers

Overview

The Data Engineers handle designing, building, and maintaining the infrastructure that allows for the collection, storage, and processing of data. They ensure that data is accessible, reliable, and ready for analysis by Data Scientists and Data Analysts.

➤ Key Responsibilities

- Data Pipeline Development: Design and implement data pipelines to collect, transform, and store data from various data sources.

- Database Management: Build and support large-scale databases and data warehouses.

- Data Integration: Integrate data from different sources and ensure data quality and consistency.

- Optimization: Refine data processing workflows for performance and scalability.

- Security: Implement data security measures and ensure compliance with data governance policies.

➤ Skills Required

- Programming Languages: Abilities in languages such as Python, Scala, and SQL.

- Data Technologies: Experience with big data technologies like Hadoop, Spark, and Kafka, as well as data warehousing solutions like Amazon Redshift, Google BigQuery, and Snowflake.

- Database Management: Knowledge of both relational (e.g., MySQL, PostgreSQL) and NoSQL (e.g., MongoDB, Cassandra) databases.

- ETL Tools: Familiarity with Extract, Transform, Load (ETL) tools like Apache NiFi, Talend, and Informatica.

- Cloud Platforms: Understanding of cloud services from providers like AWS, Azure, and Google Cloud Platform (GCP).

➤ Career Progression

1. Junior Data Engineer: Focuses on learning and supporting data pipeline development under supervision.

2. Senior Data Engineer: Takes on more complex data engineering tasks, including pipeline optimization and database management.

3. Lead Data Engineer: Leads data engineering projects, mentors junior engineers, and makes design decisions.

4. Data Engineering Manager: Oversees data engineering teams, manages projects, and aligns data strategies with business goals.

Data Scientists

Overview

Data Scientists analyse and interpret complex data to help clients and organizations make informed decisions, with calculated risks. They use statistical methods, machine learning algorithms, and data visualization techniques to extract insights from data.

➤ Key Responsibilities

- Data Analysis: Perform exploratory data analysis (EDA) to understand data patterns and relationships.

- Model Development: Develop and train machine learning models to predict outcomes and solve business problems.

- Data Visualization: Create visualizations to communicate findings and insights to stakeholders.

- Experimentation: Design and conduct POC experiments and pilots to test design and validate models.

- Collaboration: Interact with cross-functional teams to identify data-driven solutions and implement models into production.

➤ Skills Required

- Programming Languages: Deep Abilities in languages such as Python and R, to guide the team.

- Statistical Analysis: Strong understanding of statistical methods and techniques.

- Machine Learning: Experience with machine learning frameworks like TensorFlow, and PyTorch.

- Data Visualization: Knowledge of visualization tools like Tableau, Power BI

- Data Manipulation: Skills in data manipulation and cleaning using libraries like Pandas and NumPy.

- Soft Skills: Strong analytical thinking, problem-solving abilities, and communication skills.

➤ Career Progression

1. Junior Data Scientist: Focuses on data cleaning, basic analysis, and supporting senior data scientists.

2. Senior Data Scientist: Develops and implements machine learning models and collaborates on complex projects.

3. Lead Data Scientist: Leads data science projects, mentors junior scientists, and drives strategic data initiatives.

4. Data Science Manager: Manages data science teams, oversees project portfolios, and aligns data science efforts with organizational objectives.

Data Analysts

Overview

Data Analysts focus on interpreting data and generating insights to help clients and organizations make informed decisions. They primarily work with structured data and create reports and visualizations to communicate the analysed findings.

➤ Key Responsibilities

- Data Collection: Gather data from various sources and ensure data accuracy and completeness.

- Data Cleaning: Clean and preprocess data to prepare it for analysis.

- Analysis: Perform a detailed diagnostic analysis to identify trends, patterns, and anomalies.

- Reporting: Create reports and dashboards to present insights to clients and stakeholders.

- Business Insights: Translate data findings into actionable business recommendations.

➤ Skills Required

- Data Manipulation: Proficiency in SQL and data manipulation tools like Excel.

- Data Visualization: Experience with visualization tools such as Tableau, and Power BI.

- Statistical Analysis: Basic understanding of statistical methods and their application in business contexts.

- Programming: Knowledge of scripting languages like Python or R for data analysis.

- Soft Skills: Attention to detail, critical thinking, and effective communication skills.

➤ Career Progression

1. Junior Data Analyst: Focuses on data cleaning, basic analysis, and report generation under supervision.

2. Senior Data Analyst: Takes on more complex analysis tasks, creates advanced visualizations, and collaborates with other teams.

3. Lead Data Analyst: Leads analysis for projects, mentors junior analysts, and provides strategic insights and decision-making.

4. Data Analytics Manager: Manages analytics teams, oversees reporting and analysis efforts, and aligns data analysis outcomes with organizational business strategy.

Conclusion

The field of data science and analytics is growing and offers various opportunities for IT professionals. The Data Engineers, Data Scientists, and Data Analysts play crucial roles in transforming raw data into valuable insights, driving informed decision-making, and fostering innovation. By developing the necessary skills and gaining experience, IT professionals can build rewarding careers in this dynamic and expanding field.

Rise of AI and Machine Learning Specialists

The fields of Artificial Intelligence (AI) and Machine Learning (ML) are rapidly transforming industries, driving innovations, and creating new opportunities for IT professionals. AI and ML specialists are at the forefront of this revolution, developing intelligent systems and algorithms that enable machines to learn from data, make decisions, and perform tasks systematically and automatically, that traditionally required human intelligence and interference. We shall refer to the overview of AI and ML, the key responsibilities, skills required, career path and industrial opportunities for them.

- Artificial Intelligence (AI):

  The AI involves creating systems that can perform tasks typically requiring human intelligence. These tasks include visual perception, speech recognition, workflow-based decision-making, and language translation, among others.

- Machine Learning (ML):

  ML is a subset of AI that focuses on developing algorithms that allow computers to learn from and make predictions based on data. It involves training models on large datasets to recognize patterns and make informed decisions without being explicitly programmed for each task.

Key Responsibilities of AI and Machine Learning Specialists

a. Data Collection and Preparation:

- Gather and preprocess large datasets to ensure data quality and relevance.

- Clean and format data for training and testing machine learning models.

b. Model Development and Training:

- Develop, implement, and train machine learning models using various algorithms and techniques.

- Optimize models for accuracy, performance, and scalability.

c. Algorithm Selection and Implementation:

- Select appropriate algorithms for specific tasks and datasets.

- Implement algorithms using programming languages and frameworks like Python, R, TensorFlow, and PyTorch.

d. Performance Evaluation:

- Evaluate model performance using metrics such as accuracy, precision, recall, and F1-score.

- Fine-tune models based on evaluation results to improve performance.

e. Deployment and Integration:

- Deploy machine learning models into production environments.

- Integrate models with existing systems and applications.

f. Research and Innovation:

- Stay updated with the latest advancements in AI and ML.

- Research to develop new algorithms and improve existing ones.

Skills Required for AI and Machine Learning Specialists

a. Programming Languages:

- Proficiency in languages like Python, R, Java, and C++.

b. Frameworks for Machine Learning:

- Experience with frameworks such as TensorFlow, Keras, PyTorch, and Scikit-learn.

c. Data Handling and Preprocessing:

- Skills in data manipulation and preprocessing using tools like Pandas and NumPy.

d. Knowledge of Algorithms:

- Understanding of various machine learning algorithms, including supervised, unsupervised, and reinforced learning.

e. Evaluation and Optimization of Model:

- Expertise in evaluating model performance and fine-tuning hyperparameters.

f. Domain Knowledge:

- Knowledge of the specific domain where AI and ML are applied, such as healthcare, finance, or E-commerce.

Career Path and Progression

a. Entry-Level Roles:

- Machine Learning Engineer: Focus on building and deploying ML models.

- AI Research Assistant: Assist in researching and developing new AI techniques and applications.

b. Senior Roles:

- Senior Machine Learning Engineer: Lead ML projects, optimize models and mentor junior engineers.

- AI Specialist: Develop advanced AI solutions and integrate them into business processes.

c. Scientist-Level Roles:

- Data Scientist: Combine expertise in AI, ML, and domain knowledge to fetch insights from data.

- AI Research Scientist: Conduct cutting-edge research and publish findings in academic journals.

d. Leadership Roles:

- AI Architect: Design and oversee the implementation of AI systems and strategies.

- Chief AI Officer (CAIO): Lead AI initiatives, align AI strategies with business goals, and drive Innovation.

Industry-level AI Applications and Opportunities

The various applications of AI in the industry can be explored.

1. Healthcare:

- Developing AI-driven diagnostic tools and personalized treatment plans.

- Analysing medical images and predicting disease outcomes.

2. Finance:

- Implementing AI algorithms for fraud detection and risk assessment.

- Enhancing trading strategies and customer service through AI-driven chatbots.

3. Retail and E-commerce:

- Personalizing customer experiences with recommendation systems.

- Optimizing supply chain and inventory management using predictive analytics.

4. Automotive:

   - Advancing autonomous vehicle technologies with computer vision and sensor fusion.

   - Enhancing driver assistance systems and predictive maintenance.

5. Manufacturing:

   - Improving quality control with AI-powered image recognition.

   - Streamlining production processes through predictive maintenance and demand forecasting.

Conclusion

The growing career opportunities in AI and Machine Learning are creating lucrative opportunities for IT professionals. By achieving expertise in AI and ML, IT professionals can drive innovation across various industries, solve complex problems, and contribute to advancements in technology. With the growing demand for intelligent systems and data-driven decision-making, AI and ML specialists will lead the future of technological growth and make a significant impact on the IT Industry.

Careers in Cloud Computing and DevOps

Cloud Computing and DevOps are integral to modern IT infrastructure, emphasizing flexibility, scalability, and efficient operations. The professionals in these areas work to optimize the deployment, management, and reliability of applications and systems.

You would be interested in knowing the roles and growth paths in the cloud areas. Key roles within these fields include Cloud Architects, DevOps Engineers, and Site Reliability Engineers (SREs). We will have an overview of these with key responsibilities, skills required and career paths.

Cloud Architects

Overview

Cloud Architects design and manage cloud computing strategies and solutions. They work with cloud platforms (such as AWS, Azure, Google, and IBM Cloud) to build scalable, reliable, and secure cloud environments that meet an organization's needs.

➤ Key Responsibilities

- Cloud Strategy: Develop cloud adoption strategies, including selecting appropriate cloud services and defining migration plans.

- Architecture Design: Design cloud infrastructure architectures that align with business goals and technical requirements.

- Implementation: Oversee the deployment of cloud solutions, ensuring they meet performance, security, and scalability requirements.

- Optimization: Continuously optimize cloud resources for cost-efficiency and performance tuning.

- Security and Compliance: Implement security best practices and ensure compliance with relevant regulations and standards.

- Collaboration: Work with other IT professionals to integrate cloud solutions with existing systems and applications.

➤ Skills Required

- Cloud Platforms: Expertise in major cloud platforms (AWS, Azure, Google, IBM Cloud).

- Architecture Design: Strong cloud architecture and design skills, Cloud principles and best practices.

- Security: Deep Knowledge of cloud security practices and compliance requirements.

- Programming: Skills in scripting languages (Python, Bash) for automation and orchestration.

- Networking: Understanding of cloud networking and connectivity.

➤ Career Progression

1. Cloud Architect: Assists in designing and deploying cloud solutions under the guidance of senior architects.

2. Senior Cloud Architect: Leads the design and implementation of complex cloud environments.

3. Enterprise Cloud Architect: Oversees large-scale cloud projects, develops strategic cloud roadmaps, and mentors junior architects.

4. Cloud Solutions Architect: Provides high-level cloud strategy and leadership, aligning cloud initiatives with business objectives.

DevOps Engineers

Overview

DevOps Engineers have a pivotal role between development and operations, focusing on improving the software development lifecycle through automation, continuous integration/continuous delivery (CI/CD), and monitoring.

➤ Key Responsibilities

- Cloud CI/CD Pipelines: Design and implement CI/CD pipelines to automate the build, test, and deployment processes.

- Automation: Automate routine tasks and processes to improve efficiency and reduce errors.

- Monitoring and Logging: Monitoring and logging solutions Implementation to ensure system health and performance.

- Collaboration: Collaborate with development, QA, and operations teams to streamline workflows and resolve issues.

- Infrastructure as Code (IaC): Use IaC tools (e.g., Terraform, Ansible) to manage and provision infrastructure.

➤ Skills Required

- CI/CD Tools: Experience with CI/CD tools like Jenkins, GitLab CI, or CircleCI.

- Automation: Proficiency in automation tools and scripting languages (Python, Bash).

- Version Control: Knowledge of version control systems (e.g., GitHub).

- Containerization: Experience with containerization technologies (Docker) and orchestration (Kubernetes).

- Infrastructure as Code: Skills in IaC tools (Terraform, Ansible).

➤ Career Progression

1. DevOps Engineer: Supports DevOps activities, assists in pipeline creation, and automates tasks under supervision.

2. Senior Engineer: Manages CI/CD pipelines, automates infrastructure, and resolves operational issues.

3. Lead DevOps Engineer: Leads DevOps initiatives, optimizes workflows, and mentors junior engineers.

4. DevOps Manager: Oversees DevOps teams, aligns DevOps practices with organizational goals, and drives strategic improvements.

Site Reliability Engineers (SRE's)

Overview

Site Reliability Engineers focus on maintaining and improving the reliability, availability, and performance of systems and applications. They apply software engineering tools and techniques to operations tasks, blending development and operations responsibilities.

➤ Key Responsibilities

- Reliability Engineering: Ensure system reliability and availability through proactive monitoring, incident management, and performance tuning.

- Incident Response: Respond to and resolve incidents, conduct Root Cause analysis, and implement preventive measures.

- Performance Optimization: Analyse system performance and optimize infrastructure to meet service-level objectives (SLOs).

- Automation: Automate operational tasks and improve system scalability and resilience.

- Capacity Planning: Plan and manage system capacity to handle varying loads of client usage and proactively avoid outages.

➤ Skills Required

- Monitoring and Observability: Proficiency in monitoring and observability tools (Prometheus, Grafana, ELK Stack)

- Incident Management: Experience with incident response and management processes.

- Performance Tuning: Skills in optimizing system performance and reliability.

- Automation: Knowledge of automation tools and scripting languages (Python, Bash).

- Systems Design: Understanding of distributed systems and their challenges.

➤ Career Progression

1. SRE: Assists in monitoring and incident management and supports IT reliability initiatives under supervision.

2. Senior Site Reliability Engineer: Manages reliability tasks, optimizes system performance, and handles incident responses.

3. Lead SRE: Leads reliability projects, mentors junior engineers, and drives improvements in system reliability and performance.

4. SRE Manager: Oversees SRE teams, sets reliability goals and strategies, and aligns SRE practices with business objectives.

Conclusion

Cloud computing and DevOps are essential components of modern IT operations. Key roles such as Cloud Architects, DevOps Engineers, and Site Reliability Engineers are vital for managing and optimizing infrastructure and applications. These positions provide diverse opportunities for IT professionals to enhance system performance, scalability, and efficiency. By developing expertise in cloud platforms, automation, and reliability engineering, IT professionals can build successful careers in these dynamic and rapidly evolving fields. The growth in this area is expected to increase significantly in the coming years.

Careers in IT Product Development

IT product development is the entire process of designing, creating, and marketing new products or enhancing existing products with new features, useful to the clients. The IT product development focuses on technology-based products within the Information Technology industry.

From a business point of view, the purpose of IT product development is to address consumer demand to foster, maintain and increase a company's market share. While for a customer, it's to serve the business value with quality and service. There are various models for IT Product Development, essentially comprised of mentioned steps.

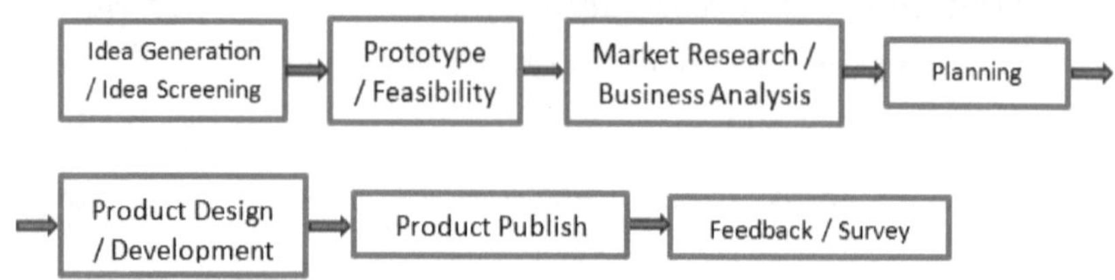

Idea Generation / Idea Screening: At the initial stage of the product development, various Ideas and opportunities are explored, to address any gap in the market or the existing product. With Idea Screening, objective assessment is carried out to filter the flawed or less desirable product ideas.

Prototype-Feasibility: A prototype is created based on the IT product concept and features, with validation of the technology stack to be used. This involves an organizational group to beta test the prototype. It is then tested with a customer base. This also determines if the IT product and features have the potential to be attainable, and viable. Further development of the concept and features is done based on the feedback.

Market Research-Business Analysis: An optimum way to market and sell a product is evaluated. This would depend on whether it is a new IT Product or an enhancement to an existing one. The market strategy can be based on the IT product and its features, price range, and target clients. The business analysis helps evaluate the mode of marketing and profitable way of selling.

Planning: The overall planning for the IT product design and development along with marketing and selling strategy is created at this stage. The more time spent on planning the lifecycle of the IT product, the better the outcome with zeroing out the post-production issues.

Product Design-Development: Usually Agile IT Product development process is followed. The Most Viable Product (MVP) features are identified and prioritized for design and development in iterative cycles. The 80/20 rule is applied to have 80% features/enhancements to be achieved with 20% of the effort and optimize the delivery cycle.

Product Publish: During the product development cycle, this would include a freeze of the IT product development cycle with completion of Integration, Regression and Acceptance testing. On the commercial side, the product is introduced to the target market, based on the strategy decided for marketing and selling.

Feedback – Survey: As the IT product is published, the product lifecycle begins. The life of the product is shaped by the response of the target market, the competition and similar products it's up against, and subsequent enhancements to the product. The customer feedback drives the further growth and path for the IT product. A survey is a good tool to get an insight into the client's mind.

We can have a look at some of the major IT Product companies and their products. There is enormous strength and scope for opportunities in this area.

IT Product Company	IT Products
Microsoft	MS Cloud, Security, Dynamic 365, Microsoft Industry, Office 365
Amazon	World's largest enterprise retailer and Cloud service provider (AWS)
Google	Search engines, Cloud computing, Hardware, YouTube
Intel	Xeon Scalable Processors, Intel Core, Pentium
Meta	Facebook, Whatsapp, Instagram
Apple	PCs (iMac), smartphones (iPhone), tablets (iPad), computer peripherals
IBM	IBM - Watsonx, Instana, Maximo, Cloud Pak, Cognos Analytics, Planning Analytics, Websphere, RPA, Consulting Advantage, Quantum Safe

IT Product Company	IT Products
Salesforce	Salesforce Platform, Sales Cloud, Service Cloud, Mulesoft, Tableau, Slack
TCS	Omnistore, BaNCS, Quartz, Mastercraft, Optumera, ignio, Chroma

(*) The Organization and Products mentioned are trademarks of the respective companies.

You would be curious to know the opportunities and roles available in the IT product development career path. We shall review the important roles in IT Product Development like UX Designer and IT Product Manager. These roles are pivotal for the product development.

UX Designer:

Overview:

The role of a User Experience (UX) Designer is to make a product or service easy to use and access. The products and services should be easy, effective, and delightful. The UX designer professional most often is associated with digital design for websites and applications. They optimize the interaction between end clients and products.

➤ Key Responsibilities

- Understand the product and client needs – Interface with the client and know the requirements. UX comprises the overall experience a user has with a product

- Conduct user study - Identify user needs, objectives, actions, and challenges.

- Create prototypes – Provide insight into the product with wireframes, sitemaps, prototypes

- Design the product – product outcome to be designed elegantly to satisfy the market

➤ Skills Required

- Innovative Analytics – The mind should be tuned to innovation with analytics.

- Prototyping, Wireframing – Technical skills to create the partial features for client demos.

- Communication – Interface with stakeholders requires high collaboration.

- Google UX Design Professional Certificate can be one starting point for the career start.

➤ Career Progression

1. Product designer - Responsible for the entire product collaborating with teams and Creating visual designs.

2. UX design specialization - A technical path with an individual specializing in specific areas.

3. UX Manager – The Management path for the design delivery management

4. Consultant – The Free Lance path to work independently.

IT Product Manager

Overview

A Product manager identifies opportunities, empathizes with users, and collaborates with others. This is a techno-managerial role, so the professional should understand technology as well as the product and clients.

➤ Key Responsibilities

- Develop innovative products – The industry-leading features should be identified to drive innovative product lines.

- Identify opportunities – Carry out market research with the teams, and explore prospect

- Drive the strategy, and manage delivery schedule – Based on market needs decide tactics and manage the design and development cycles.

- Motivate cross-functional teams – As there are multiple domain teams involved, collaborate and encourage the various teams.

- Influence key stakeholders – The client stakeholders are important decision-makers, those should be influenced, managing the expectations.

➤ Skills Required

- User-Centric Design Approach - Align with the users, addressing needs and expectations.

- Product Development Lifecycle - Knowledge of the entire product development lifecycle

- Leadership and Interpersonal Skills - Ability to lead and interact effectively with others.

- Product management – Agile Scrum mastery with prioritization, leading the market with innovation, strategic planning and immaculate execution.

➤ Career Progression

1. Associate Product Manager – Initial phase of a career supporting the Senior management.

2. Product Manager – Overall responsibility for the product design and delivery.

3. Senior Product Manager – Extending ownership with market research, strategic design and client-centric delivery, requires deep product and market knowledge, managing stakeholders and higher management.

4. Director of Product – Define Product strategy, Develop and drive product roadmap, Engage with customers and partners, and Drive lifecycle as a product owner.

Conclusion

The IT Product Development is evolving as a niche area. There would be ample opportunities in this area. By understanding the key differences and evaluating personal aspirations and career goals, IT professionals can make informed choices and embark on a fulfilling career path in IT Product Development and Management. That will help satisfy their career aspirations and growth.

Glance at IT Business in the World

Gartner US, the most trusted research-based business advisory organisation, publishes in-depth analysed IT business reports, that give insight and trends of the IT business in the world.

Worldwide enterprise software revenue totalled $785.1 billion in 2023, with an 11.0% year-over-year growth rate. Analytics platforms emerged as the fastest-growing market, with a 14.4% growth rate. Microsoft, Oracle and Amazon continued to be the leading providers for 2023. (Gartner report: 22 April 2024)

Gartner Survey shows 85% of Business Leaders agree there will be a surge in skills development needs due to AI and Digital Trends in the next 3 years. (Gartner report: 29 October 2024).

As digital and AI trends continue to disrupt work, the need for skills development will dramatically increase. The organizations will have to ensure their workforce has the time and resources to continuously learn, and remain technically and physically fit to deliver the ever-growing business. In the context of today's AI-fuelled accelerated disruption, learning and development are quite slow to respond to the volume, variety and velocity of skills needs. Learning and Development must become more agile to respond to changes faster and deliver learning more rapidly and more cost-effectively.

IT industry employment statistics reveal evolving trends. The number of employed people in the IT sector varies across regions based on infrastructure and budgetary allocations. Automation and intelligent technologies mould the future of IT business and employment, streamlining processes, although ongoing basis requiring skill-set shifts.

The future of the IT industry and employment looks bright, but it needs to be explored properly with the right directional efforts, tracking industry trends and evolving skill requirements over time.

Chapter 4

Essential Skills for IT Professionals

As the IT industry is becoming mature and stable, role-wise certain technical skills, along with soft skills and leadership are expected to be present with the IT Professional. We will have a detailed look at the technical skills, soft skills and allied skills like problem-solving, critical thinking, and growth mindset among others.

Technical Skills: Programming Languages, Tools, and Technologies

We will provide a comprehensive description for IT professionals regarding essential technical skills, emphasizing programming languages, tools, and technologies.

Key Programming Languages

Java

- Overview: Java is a class-based, object-oriented programming language designed for portability and performance. Being platform-independent, Java has become the industry standard.

- Applications: Enterprise applications, Android app development, web applications (Spring), large-scale systems.

- Key Features: Platform independence (JVM), strong memory management, robust security features.

JavaScript

- Overview: JavaScript is a versatile, high-level programming language primarily used for web development.

- Applications: Front-end development (React, Angular, Vue.js), back-end development (Node.js), mobile app development (React Native), serverless applications.

- Key Features: Asynchronous programming, event-driven, integration with HTML/CSS.

C#

- Overview: C# is a modern, object-oriented programming language developed by Microsoft, part of the .NET ecosystem.

- Applications: Windows applications, web development (ASP.NET), game development (Unity), enterprise solutions.

- Key Features: Strong type-checking, integration with .NET libraries, support for asynchronous programming.

SQL

- Overview: SQL (Structured Query Language) is used for managing and manipulating relational databases.

- Applications: Database management, data analysis, reporting, backend development.

- Key Features: Querying, inserting, updating, and deleting data, transaction control, indexing.

Python

- Overview: Python is a high-level, interpreted language known for its simplicity and readability.

- Applications: Web development (Django, Flask), data science (Pandas, NumPy), machine learning (TensorFlow, Scikit-learn), automation, scripting.

- Key Features: Dynamic typing, extensive libraries, and frameworks, strong community support.

Essential Tools and Platforms

AWS (Amazon Web Services)

- Overview: AWS is a comprehensive and widely adopted cloud platform offering over 200+ fully featured services from data centres, available globally.

- Key Services: EC2 (compute), S3 (storage), RDS (relational database service), Lambda (serverless computing).

- Applications: Hosting applications, data storage and analysis, machine learning, IoT.

  e.g. The Cricket IPL Matches held in India were hosted and workload managed on the AWS platform.

Azure

- Overview: Microsoft Azure is a cloud computing service providing a wide range of services for building, deploying, and managing applications.

- Key Services: Virtual Machines, Azure SQL Database, Azure DevOps, Azure Functions (serverless computing).

- Applications: Hybrid cloud solutions, AI and machine learning, analytics, DevOps.

  e.g. Various medium to large business applications are hosted with the Azure cloud platform.

IBM Cloud

- Overview: IBM Public Cloud is a cloud computing service with a hybrid cloud, driving cost efficiency, increased productivity, sustainability and faster time to market. Applying generative AI to IT automation can accelerate that journey even faster.

- Key Services: Hybrid cloud architecture, Cloud Accelerator platform, DB2, Cloudant, DevOps, IBM Garage.

- Applications: Primarily Enterprise Applications. IBM is named a Leader in the 2024 Gartner Magic Quadrant for Public Cloud and IT Transformation Services.

Docker

- Overview: Docker is a platform for developing, shipping, and running applications in containers.

- Key Features: Containerization, isolation of applications, portability across different environments.

- Applications: Microservices architecture, continuous integration/ continuous deployment (CI/CD), development and testing.

Kubernetes

- Overview: Kubernetes is an open-source platform for automating deployment, scaling, and operations of application containers.

- Key Features: Container orchestration, load balancing, self-healing, scaling.

- Applications: Managing containerized applications, cloud-native applications, DevOps.

Git and GitHub

- Overview: Git is a distributed version control system, and GitHub is a web-based platform for version control and collaboration.

- Key Features: Branching and merging, code review, issue tracking, CI/CD integration with Cloud services.

- Applications: Source code management, collaborative development, open-source projects.

GitHub Copilot

- GitHub Copilot is an AI coding assistant that helps to write code faster and with less effort, allowing a professional to focus more energy on problem-solving and collaboration. GitHub Copilot has been proven to increase developer productivity and accelerate the pace of software development.

Jenkins

- Overview: Jenkins is an open-source automation server for building, testing, and deploying code.

- Key Features: Pipeline as code, extensible with plugins, distributed builds.

- Applications: CI/CD pipelines, automated testing, DevOps practices.

Terraform

- Overview: Terraform is an open-source infrastructure as code (IaC) software tool created by HashiCorp.

- Key Features: Declarative configuration files, infrastructure provisioning, multi-cloud support.

- Applications: Automated infrastructure management, cloud provisioning, versioned infrastructure.

Conclusion

For IT professionals, mastering key programming languages and becoming familiar with essential tools, techniques, and platforms is crucial for effective performance and career advancement in various IT roles. Learning and adapting to the latest technologies while continuously enhancing technical skills can significantly boost an IT professional's ability to innovate, optimize, and secure IT systems and applications. This commitment to growth not only contributes to personal development but also helps achieve the business goals of clients and organizations.

Soft Skills: Communication, Leadership, and Teamwork

Soft skills play a pivotal role in the career of an IT Professional. The good part of it is that soft skills can be developed over time, with training, coaching and practicing. To rise on the leadership ladder, soft skills should be emphatically developed.

Communication

Importance: Effective communication is crucial in IT for ensuring clarity, fostering collaboration, and avoiding misunderstandings that can lead to project delays or failures. A professional having better communication always moves ahead on the ladder, getting more productive results. So, always refine your communication skills, to help progress your career graph.

Paul J. Meyer, a pioneer in the personal development industry said "Communication – the human connection – is the key to personal and career success."

You would be vouching for enhancing your communication skills. We shall see various communication techniques, to be adopted for betterment.

Effective Communication Techniques

a. Activue Listening:

- Description: Fully concentrate on what is being said rather than just passively hearing the Message.

- Benefits: Builds trust, ensures understanding, and helps to identify key issues.

- How to Improve:

  - Maintain eye contact.

  - Nod and use facial expressions to show engagement.

  - Paraphrase or summarize what the speaker said.

b. Clarity and Conciseness:

- Description: Convey your message clearly and concisely, avoiding unnecessary jargon.

- Benefits: Reduces the risk of misunderstandings and keeps the audience engaged.

- How to Improve:
  - Think before you speak.
  - Use simple language and avoid technical jargon when communicating with non-technical Stakeholders.
  - Structure your communication with a clear beginning, middle, and end.

c. Non-Verbal Communication:

- Description: Use body language, facial expressions, and tone of voice to reinforce your Message.

- Benefits: Complements verbal communication and can convey emotions and attitudes.

- How to Improve:
  - Be mindful of your body language and ensure it matches your words.
  - Use gestures to emphasize key points.
  - Maintain an appropriate tone of voice to suit the context.

d. Feedback:

- Description: Give and receive constructive feedback to improve performance and build stronger relationships.

- Benefits: Encourages growth, enhances collaboration, and resolves issues promptly.

- How to Improve:
  - Be specific and focus on behaviours, not personalities.

- Use the "sandwich method" (positive feedback, constructive feedback, positive feedback).

- Be open to receiving feedback and use it as a learning opportunity.

Leadership

Importance: Leadership skills are essential for guiding teams, making strategic decisions, and driving projects to success in the IT Industry. Per say, 'Leaders are Born', Though Leadership can be developed as a vital skill with training, practice and coaching.

N. R. Narayana Murthy, Chairman Emeritus Infosys said "A great leader also has the ability to make people an inch taller in his presence. Leading by example is the most powerful advice you can give to anybody."

You would be looking to develop Leadership skills and here is the way to achieve it.

Developing Leadership Qualities

a. Vision and Strategic Thinking:

- Description: Ability to set a clear vision and long-term goals and create strategies to achieve them.

- Benefits: Aligns team efforts and motivates them towards common objectives.

- How to Improve:

  - Stay informed about industry trends and emerging technologies.

  - Engage in strategic planning and set measurable goals.

  - Communicate the vision clearly to the team and involve them in the planning process.

b. Decision-Making:

- Description: Ability to make informed and timely decisions that benefit the team and the organization.

- Benefits: Ensures projects stay on track and enhances team confidence.

- How to Improve:
  - Gather relevant information and consider different perspectives.
  - Weigh the pros and cons of each option.
  - Be decisive and take responsibility for the outcomes.

c. Mentorship and Coaching:

- Description: Providing guidance, support, and feedback to help team members grow professionally.

- Benefits: Enhances team skills, promotes a learning culture, and builds loyalty.

- How to Improve:
  - Offer regular one-on-one meetings with team members.
  - Provide opportunities for learning and development.
  - Share your knowledge and experiences openly.

d. Empathy and Emotional Intelligence:

- Description: Understanding and managing your own emotions and being aware of and considerate towards others' emotions.

- Benefits: Builds strong relationships, enhances team morale, and improves conflict resolution.

- How to Improve:
  - Practice active listening and show genuine interest in others' concerns.
  - Develop self-awareness and regulate your emotions.

- Show appreciation and recognize team members' contributions.

While IQ measures cognitive abilities such as problem-solving and logical reasoning, EQ encompasses the essential skills of self-awareness, self-regulation, empathy, motivation and social interaction. As remote and hybrid working options become the global norm, a need for more emotionally intelligent practices and leaders emerges. Leaders who cultivate these skills deliver better results. So, it's better to imbibe and cultivate these skills.

Teamwork

Importance: Effective teamwork ensures that projects are completed efficiently and successfully, leveraging the diverse skills and perspectives of team members.

Steve Jobs, Former CEO of Apple said "Great things in business are never done by one person."

It is the teamwork that makes the success happen. Various traits are needed to build a mature team with healthy teamwork. You would leverage it to manage the team well.

Building Strong Teamwork

a. Collaboration:

- Description: Working together towards a common goal, sharing knowledge and responsibilities.

- Benefits: Combines different skills and ideas to achieve better outcomes.

- How to Improve:

  - Foster a collaborative environment where everyone feels valued.

  - Encourage open communication and idea sharing.

- Use collaborative tools and platforms (e.g., Slack, Microsoft Teams).

b. Conflict Resolution:

- Description: Addressing and resolving disagreements constructively.

- Benefits: Maintains a positive team atmosphere and prevents disruptions.

- How to Improve:

  - Address conflicts early and openly.

  - Listen to all parties involved and understand their perspectives.

  - Work towards a mutually acceptable solution.

c. Adaptability:

- Description: Being flexible and open to change, adjusting to new roles, responsibilities, and work environments and culture.

- Benefits: Keeps the team agile and responsive to changing project requirements. Reduce the turnaround time and time to market.

- How to Improve:

  - Embrace change as an opportunity for growth.

  - Encourage a culture of continuous improvement and learning.

  - Be willing to step out of your comfort zone and take on new challenges.

Conclusion

For IT professionals, soft skills like effective communication, leadership, and teamwork are just as important as technical expertise. These skills enhance collaboration, drive project success, and create a positive work environment. By continuously developing their soft skills, IT professionals can improve their overall performance, strengthen relationships, and advance their careers. Various online training programs are available at the organizational level as well as through different institutes. These programs focus on improving communication skills, particularly public speaking, which also contributes to the development of leadership abilities.

The Importance of Problem-Solving and Critical Thinking

Analytical skills with problem-solving and critical thinking are another important area of expertise to be developed. Along with importance, we shall see the key steps and application of it.

Problem-Solving Skills

Definition: Problem-solving skills involve identifying, analysing, and resolving issues that arise, in a time-bound, methodical and effective manner.

Importance:

- Efficiency: Effective problem-solving helps in quickly identifying the root cause of issues and implementing solutions, thereby minimizing downtime and maintaining productivity.

- Innovation: Encourages creative thinking, leading to innovative solutions that can improve processes, products, and services.

- Risk Management: Helps in anticipating potential issues and developing strategies to mitigate risks before they escalate.

Key Steps in Problem-Solving

a. Identify the Problem:

- Clearly define the issue and understand its scope.

- Use tools and techniques like the 5W1H method, Fishbone Diagram, or Pareto Analysis to pinpoint the root cause.

b. Analyse the Problem:

- Gather relevant data and information to understand the problem's impact.

- Break down the problem into smaller, manageable parts.

c. Develop Solutions:

- Brainstorm potential solutions and evaluate their feasibility.

- Consider both short-term fixes and long-term solutions.

d. Implement the Solution:

- Develop an action plan and assign responsibilities.

- Ensure clear communication and monitor the implementation process.

e. Evaluate the Outcome:

- Assess the effectiveness of the solution.

- Gather feedback and adjust if necessary.

Application in IT

- Debugging and troubleshooting software issues.

- Resolving network and infrastructure problems.

- Optimizing system performance and efficiency.

- Managing project-related challenges and constraints.

Critical Thinking Skills

Definition: Critical thinking involves the objective analysis and evaluation of an issue to form a judgment, with calculated risk. It requires open-mindedness, logical reasoning, and the ability to counter assumptions. It helps in decision-making, risk-taking, and developing innovative approaches and solutions.

Importance:

- Decision-Making: Enhances the ability to make well-informed and rational decisions, leading to better project outcomes and strategic planning.

- Quality Assurance: Ensures thorough analysis and testing, reducing the likelihood of errors and improving the quality of deliverables.

- Adaptability: Helps in quickly adapting to new information and changing environments, a crucial trait in the fast-paced IT industry.

Key Components of Critical Thinking

a. Observation:

- Gather relevant information and identify patterns.

- Stay informed about industry trends and advancements.

b. Analysis:

- Break down complex problems and data into simpler components.

- Use logical reasoning to assess information and identify relationships.

c. Inference:

- Draw conclusions based on evidence and reasoning.

- Evaluate the implications and potential outcomes of different actions.

d. Evaluation:

- Critically assess arguments, solutions, and decisions.

- Consider alternative perspectives and challenge assumptions.

e. Explanation:

- Clearly and logically communicate your reasoning and conclusions.

- Provide evidence and justification for your decisions.

f. Self-Regulation:

- Reflect on your thought processes and biases.

- Continuously seek to improve your critical thinking skills.

Application in IT

- Evaluating the feasibility and impact of new technologies and solutions.

- Conducting thorough risk assessments and developing mitigation strategies.

- Designing and implementing robust and scalable systems.

- Enhancing security measures by identifying potential vulnerabilities and threats.

Conclusion

For IT professionals, problem-solving and critical thinking skills are essential for navigating the complexities and challenges of the IT industry. These skills empower professionals to effectively address issues, make informed decisions, and drive innovation. By developing strong problem-solving and critical thinking abilities, IT professionals can enhance their effectiveness, contribute to the success of their projects and organizations, and remain competitive in a rapidly evolving industry.

Building a Growth Mindset and Adaptability

A growth mindset and adaptability are other important skill areas, an individual should adopt to become a mature IT Professional. Along with the importance, we shall see how to build it.

Growth Mindset

Definition: A growth mindset is the belief that abilities and intelligence can be developed through dedication, hard work, and continuous learning.

➤ Importance

- Encourages Learning: Promotes continuous learning and skill development, crucial in the fast-paced IT industry.

- Enhances Resilience: Helps professionals bounce back from setbacks and view challenges as Growth opportunities.

- Fosters Innovation: Encourages experimentation and creative problem-solving, leading to Innovative solutions.

➤ How to Build a Growth Mindset

a. Embrace Challenges:

- View challenges as opportunities to learn and grow.

- Take on new and difficult tasks to push your boundaries.

b. Learn from Criticism:

- Accept constructive feedback as a tool for improvement.

- Reflect on feedback and use it to enhance your skills and performance.

c. Celebrate Effort:

- Focus on the effort and process, not just the outcome.

- Recognize and reward persistence and hard work.

d. Be Persistent:

- Stay motivated even when facing obstacles.

- Keep trying different approaches until you succeed.

e. Learn from Others:

- Observe and learn from the experiences and successes of your peers.

- Seek out mentors and role models who exemplify a growth mindset.

Adaptability

Definition: Adaptability is the ability to adjust to new conditions, changes, and challenges quickly and effectively.

➤ Importance

- Keeps You Relevant: Staying adaptable ensures you remain relevant in an ever-evolving technology landscape.

- Enhances Problem-Solving: Allows for more effective and creative problem-solving by being open to new approaches.

- Supports Career Growth: Adaptability is highly valued by employers and can lead to new opportunities and career advancement.

➤ How to Build Adaptability

a. Stay Informed:

- Keep up with industry trends, new technologies, and best practices.

- Follow industry news, blogs, webinars, and online courses.

b. Be Open to Change:

- Embrace change as an opportunity for improvement and innovation.

- Be willing to let go of old habits and adapt to new processes and tools.

c. Develop a Learning Plan:

- Identify areas for improvement and set learning goals.

- Invest time in acquiring new skills and knowledge regularly.

d. Seek Diverse Experiences:

- Take on different roles and responsibilities to broaden your skill set.

- Collaborate with colleagues from different departments and backgrounds.

e. Practice Flexibility:

- Be open to feedback and willing to adjust your approach based on new information.

- Stay calm and composed in the face of unexpected changes or challenges.

Embracing Change and Continuous Learning

To become proficient in the IT industry, embracing change and continuous learning are essential. We shall see how it can be achieved.

Embracing Change

- Always remain Positive: Maintain a positive attitude towards change and see it as a pathway to growth.

- Be Proactive: Anticipate changes in your industry and prepare for them in advance.

- Engage with the Change: Participate actively in change initiatives and contribute your ideas and solutions.

Continuous Learning

- Define Learning Goals: Identify skills and knowledge areas you want to learn and enhance and set specific, achievable goals. It could be monthly, quarterly, and yearly goals, and track it for completion.

- Use Various Learning Resources: Utilize online courses from the Organization or open market, certifications, books, podcasts, and workshops.

- Apply What You Learn: Implement new knowledge and skills in your daily tasks and projects to reinforce learning. If the technology may not be with your current project, opt for a stretch assignment with a sandbox environment, which would help develop and verify your skills with usage.

- Seek Feedback: Regularly get feedback for your performance and areas for improvement, from peers and managers.

- Reflect on Your Learning: Take time to reflect on what you've learned and how it has impacted your work. A self-reflection regularly helps traverse further for growth.

Conclusion

For IT professionals, developing a growth mindset and adaptability is crucial for thriving in a rapidly changing industry. Embracing change and committing to continuous learning ensure that you remain agile, innovative, and proficient in your role. By fostering a growth mindset and developing adaptability, IT professionals can enhance their problem-solving capabilities, stay current with emerging technologies, and advance in their careers.

Professional Growth Journey

The Growth journey model describes four zones through which the professional is required to progress to learn, grow, develop and achieve the objectives. The journey from comfort zone to growth zone can be challenging but would be beneficial. It requires taking risks, challenging self, overcoming fear and embracing the change.

Comfort Zone

The professional feels comfortable, safe, secure and in control. He is quite satisfied with what he knows and what he has. He may not look for change or move. There are some or no risks or concerns. One must decide to move out of comfort zone by identifying limiting beliefs, or else the growth and benefits remain limited.

Fear Zone

Once you leave your comfort zone, you will face the unknown. You may feel less confident and concerned by opine of other people. You may find excuses to not take progressive steps. Some fear factors are good for putting pressure on yourself to achieve results. But at this stage, you should develop a growth mindset with the belief that you can do it. You should link this unknown factor as your challenging but achievable goal and come out of fear to move forward.

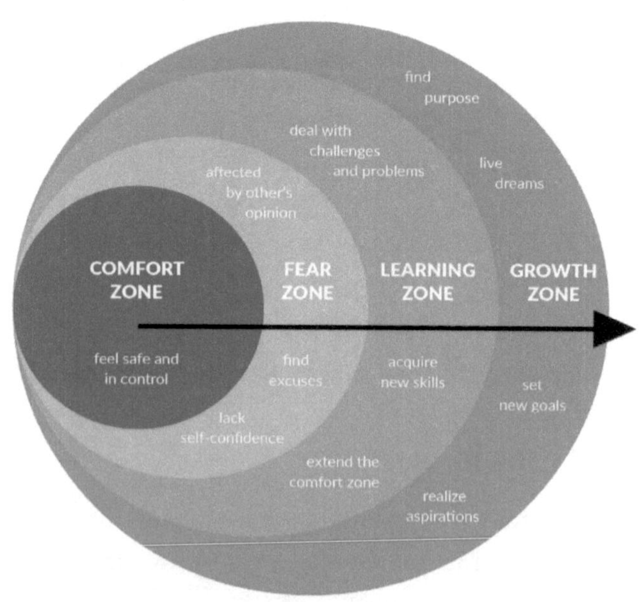

Learning Zone

This is an awaken-mind state. You will stretch yourself to learn more about current or new areas. You will acquire new skills by putting in more effort. You will be open to challenges and problems and become aware of opportunities. You may have some anxiety, but it can have a healthy impact to drive you ahead. You could take a calculated risk to push your comfort boundaries. But beware not to get into the trap of another comfort zone.

Growth Zone

Once you reach the growth zone, you will have left your comfort, have overcome all the fear factors, and be better skilled with new knowledge. You will set new goals and work towards achieving them. You will find the purpose of your job, passion and values. You will dream big for the desired future and strive for it with your full potential. The process is iterative, resulting in broader benefits to others. Further to self-growth, the professional will try to maximise the team and organization's capability, driving business growth.

Conclusion

Reaching the growth zone by stepping out of your comfort zone can be challenging, but it is also an incredibly rewarding step for your career. It requires us to push past our comfort limits, overcome fears, face challenges, and embrace change. By eliminating limiting beliefs, acquiring new skills, and setting new goals, IT professionals can focus on the connection between the Learning and Growth zones, helping them achieve their aspirations and passions.

Chapter 5

Strategic Skill Building

IT professionals should take strategic steps to build their skills effectively. There are several skillset patterns that individuals and organizations can follow for skill development. We will explore the T, PI, and Comb patterns to help you enhance your skill set and advance your career. You can develop your skillsets or those of your team to shape individual career opportunities, and to shape the skill patterns for your organization.

- (T) A beginner would start with a 'T' shaped skillset building pattern. With this pattern, you will get a broad understanding of the business domain, that's a horizontal line; while you will also develop deep skills, as a specialist or expert in one of the skill areas from the domain. That's the vertical line of the T. The type of skill can be as per your skillset - technical managerial or leadership.

- (**π**) An experienced person would acquire a 'PI' shaped skill set. In this pattern, you would continue to have further broader understanding of the entire domain or work stream or system; In addition, you would develop skill depth in two main areas from your domain. Eg If you have Java Development as a deep skill in T shape pattern while developing broad skills/knowledge in your domain; you will now develop Infrastructure Administration as one other area of expertise. In this way, you can develop a 'PI' skill set pattern.

- (▐�▌) With the 'COMB' skill shape pattern, you will develop an extended broad base of domain knowledge as part of the top of the comb. You would also develop multiple expertise areas which gives the shape of a comb. eg. Enterprise Architect or an Executive Manager can have a COMB-shaped skills expertise, with deep strength in multiple skill areas, having broad perspectives of the industry and domains.

Identifying and Assessing Skill Gaps

We shall see how the skill gaps can be identified, assess the gaps, create an Action Plan to close these and track it for completion.

Identifying Skill Gaps

Definition: Skill gaps are the difference between the skills you currently possess, and the skills required to perform your job effectively or advance in your career.

Importance:

- Career Development: Identifying skill gaps helps in creating a targeted development plan to advance your career.

- Improved Performance: Closing skill gaps can lead to better job performance and increased productivity.

- Staying Competitive: Ensuring your skills are up to date with industry standards helps you remain competitive in the job market and peer competitiveness.

Steps to Identify Skill Gaps

a. Review Job Requirements:

- Analyse Job Descriptions: Look at current and desired job roles to understand the required skills and competencies.

- Benchmark Against Industry Standards: Compare your skills with industry standards and trends.

b. Gather Feedback:

- Seek Input from Managers and Peers: Ask for feedback on your performance and areas where you could improve or enhance skills.

- Conduct Performance Reviews: Regular performance evaluations can highlight strengths and areas for development. Seek for Coach for your career growth, who can advise you on the steps to be taken.

c. Self-Assessment:

- Reflect on Your Experiences: Think about past projects and identify any challenges you faced due to lacking specific skills.

- Set Personal Goals: Align your skills with your career goals and identify skill gaps that need to be filled to achieve these goals, with training or certifications.

Assessing Skill Gaps

We shall look at various Self-Assessment Tools and Techniques. You could implement it in your day-to-day life to improve your skills and way of working.

- Skills Gap Matrix

  - **Description:** A comprehensive list of skills you currently possess, categorized by technical, soft,   Domain-specific skills, project management skills, Leadership skills, and Executive skills.

  - **How to Use:**

    - Create a detailed list of your skills.

    - Rate your proficiency in each skill on a scale (e.g., 1 to 5, or as Low, Medium, High or New, Basic, Experienced, Expert, Thought Leader).

    - Identify skills that are critical for your current or desired job but are rated at a lower level.

- ➤ The Skills Gap Analysis Template - refer to Annexure B-1.

- SWOT Analysis

  - **Description:** Analysing your Strengths, Weaknesses, Opportunities, and Threats to gain insight into your skills.

  - **How to Use:**

    - Strengths: List the skills that you have, and you want to excel at.

    - Weaknesses: Identify areas where you have a lack of proficiency.

    - Opportunities: Look for skills that can open new career opportunities for you.

    - Threats: Identify external factors that might constrain your skill development or job performance.

- ➤ The SWOT Template - refer to Annexure B-2.

- Organizational Competency Frameworks

  - **Description:** Structured models that outline the skills and behaviours required for specific roles or career paths.

- **How to Use:**
  - Identify the competency framework relevant to your industry or role.
  - Assess your current skills against the framework.
  - Highlight areas where you meet or exceed expectations and those where you fall short.
- 360-Degree Feedback
  - **Description:** A feedback process where you receive anonymous input from reporting people, peers, subordinates, supervisors, and sometimes clients.
  - **How to Use:**
    - Request feedback from a diverse group of colleagues. It could be in a digital form way.
    - Analyse the feedback to identify recurring themes and areas for improvement.
    - Use the insights to create a targeted development plan for yourself.
- Online Assessment Tools
  - **Description:** Web-based platforms that offer assessments and quizzes to evaluate your skills.
  - **Examples:**
    - LinkedIn Skills Assessments: Short quizzes to validate your skills and showcase them on your profile.
    - Coursera and Udemy: Pre-assessment tests before starting a course.
    - Pluralsight: Offers Skill IQ assessments to measure your proficiency in various technical skills.

- How to Use:

  - Take assessments related to your current or desired skills.

  - Review the results to understand your proficiency levels and areas needing improvement.

- Action Plan for Closing Skill Gaps

  a. Set SMART Goals:

     - **S**pecific: Clearly define what skill you want to develop.

     - **M**easurable: Determine how you will measure your progress.

     - **A**chievable: Ensure the goal is realistic and attainable.

     - **R**elevant: Align the goal with your career objectives.

     - **T**ime-bound: Set a deadline for achieving the goal.

  b. Create a Learning Plan:

     - Enrol in Courses: Take online courses, attend workshops, or pursue certifications relevant to your skill gaps.

     - On-the-Job Training: Seek opportunities to apply new skills in your current role.

     - Mentorship: Find a mentor who can provide guidance and support in your skill development journey.

  c. Regularly Review and Upgrade:

     - Track Progress: Monitor your progress regularly and adjust your learning plan as needed.

     - Seek Feedback: Continuously seek feedback from peers and managers to gauge improvement.

     - Stay Updated: Keep up with industry trends and emerging technologies to ensure your skills remain relevant.

Conclusion

For IT professionals, identifying and assessing skill gaps is a crucial step toward personal and career development. By utilizing self-assessment tools and techniques, you can gain a clear understanding of your current skill set, evaluate your proficiency levels, and identify any skill gaps. This process allows you to pinpoint areas for improvement and create a targeted development plan to address these gaps within a specific timeline. By following this proactive approach, you can enhance your job performance and position yourself for long-term career success in the ever-evolving IT industry.

Creating an Individual Development Plan (IDP)

An Individual Development Plan is a structured approach to identifying and achieving your learning and development goals. It helps you focus on areas that need improvement and track your progress with a plan over the planned timeline. We will see the steps to create IDP and setting up smart goals.

Steps to Create an Individual Development Plan

a. Self-Assessment:

- Identify Skills and Knowledge: Start by listing your current skills and knowledge. Use self-assessment tools and techniques (like skills inventory, SWOT analysis, and competency frameworks) to understand your strengths and areas for improvement.

- Define Your Career Goals: Determine where you want to be in your career in the short term (1-2 years) and long term (3-5 years).

b. Identify Skill Gaps:

- Compare Current Skills to Desired Skills: Look at the skills required for your desired roles and compare them with your current skill set to identify gaps.

- Prioritize Skill Gaps: Rank the skill gaps based on their importance and relevance to your career goals.

c. Research Learning Resources:

- Online Courses and Certifications: Platforms like Coursera, Udemy, Pluralsight, LinkedIn Learning, and edX offer courses tailored to various IT skills.

- Books and Articles: Identify key books, blogs, and articles that can deepen your knowledge.

- Workshops and Conferences: Attend industry events, workshops, and conferences to learn from experts and network with peers.

- On-the-Job Learning: Look for opportunities to take on projects or tasks that will help you develop the skills you need.

d. Set SMART Goals:

- Specific: Clearly define what you want to achieve.

- Measurable: Determine how you will measure your progress.

- Achievable: Ensure the goal is realistic and within your capabilities.

- Relevant: Align the goal with your career objectives.

- Time-bound: Set a deadline for achieving the goal.

e. Develop a Learning Schedule:

- Weekly/Daily Learning Time: Dedicate specific times each week or day for learning activities.

- Milestones and Checkpoints: Break down your goals into smaller milestones and set checkpoints to review your progress.

f. Implement and Track Progress:

- Start Learning: Begin with your prioritized skill gaps and use the resources you've identified.

- Track Progress: Keep a record of your learning activities and progress toward your goals.

- Adjust as Needed: Be flexible and adjust your plan based on your progress and any changes in your career goals or job requirements.

Setting SMART Goals for Skill Development

The SMART goals provide a clear and actionable framework for setting and achieving your skill development objectives.

- Components of SMART Goals

  a. **S**pecific:

    - Example: Instead of saying "I want to learn programming," please be specific and specify that "I want to learn Python programming."

  b. **M**easurable:

    - Example: "I will complete the 'Python for Everybody' specialization on Coursera and build three projects using Python."

  c. **A**chievable:

    - Example: "I will dedicate 5 hours a week to studying Python," ensuring that the goal is realistic given your current commitments.

  d. **R**elevant:

    - Example: "Learning Python will help me transition to a backend developer role, which aligns with my career goals."

e. **T**ime-bound:

  - Example: "I will complete the Python specialization and projects within 3 months."

- Examples of SMART Goals for IT Professionals

a. Technical Skills:

  - Goal: I will become proficient in cloud computing by earning the AWS Certified Solutions Architect certification within 6 months.

  - Action Plan: Enrol in an AWS training course, study 4 hours per week, and schedule the certification exam, within a month.

b. Soft Skills:

  - Goal: I will improve my communication skills by attending a public speaking workshop and delivering three presentations at team meetings over the next 4 months.

  - Action Plan: Register for the workshop, practice presentations, and seek feedback from your manager and colleagues.

c. Project Management:

  - Goal: I will enhance my project management skills by completing the PMP certification within 8 months.

  - Action Plan: Enrol in a PMP prep course, study 10 hours per week, and take practice exams.

d. Coding and Development:

  - Goal: I will learn JavaScript and build a portfolio of 5 web applications within the next 6 months.

  - Action Plan: Complete an online JavaScript course, follow tutorials, and work on projects during weekends.

e. Networking:

- Goal: I will expand my professional network by attending at least 4 industry conferences and joining 2 professional IT associations within the next year.

- Action Plan: Research and register for conferences, participate in association events, and actively engage in networking opportunities.

➤ Individual Development Plan (IDP) Template - refer to Annexure B-3.

Conclusion

Developing an Individual Development Plan (IDP) and setting SMART goals are crucial steps for IT professionals who want to advance their careers. By identifying skill gaps, establishing specific and actionable goals, and following a structured learning schedule, you can ensure continuous growth and development in the constantly evolving IT industry. This proactive approach not only improves your technical and soft skills but also prepares you for long-term career success.

Leveraging Online Courses and Certifications

We shall study the importance of online courses, certifications, the top platforms that can be referred to, and how they can be explored for our progress.

Importance of Online Courses and Certifications

a. Continuous Learning:

- The IT industry is constantly evolving with new technologies, frameworks, and tools. Online courses and certifications help professionals stay updated with the latest trends and advancements.

b. Career Advancement:

- Certifications and advanced courses can enhance your resume, making you more competitive in the job market. They demonstrate your commitment to professional development and your expertise in specific areas.

c. Flexibility and Accessibility:

- Online learning platforms provide flexibility to learn at your own pace and schedule, making it easier to balance learning with work and other commitments.

d. Skill Validation:

- Certifications validate your skills and knowledge, providing proof of your expertise to employers and peers.

Top Platforms for IT Learning

We shall refer to some of the well-known IT Learning platforms, which can assure good quality training and industrial certifications.

a. Coursera

Overview

Coursera partners with top universities and organizations to offer online courses, specializations, and degrees across various fields, including IT and computer science. It partners.

e.g. with IBM, Microsoft, Google, well known US Universities among others.

Key Features

- Wide Range of Courses: Courses on programming, data science, AI, cloud computing, cybersecurity, and more.

- Certifications and Degrees: Professional certificates, specializations, and even full degrees from reputed institutions.

- Flexible Learning: Self-paced learning options and deadlines to fit your schedule.

- Practical Projects: Many courses include hands-on projects to apply your learning.

Popular Courses

- Google IT Support Professional Certificate
- IBM Data Science Professional Certificate
- Machine Learning by Stanford University

b. Udemy

Overview

Udemy is a global marketplace for learning and teaching online, with a vast selection of courses on various topics, including IT and software development.

Key Features

- Diverse Course Selection: Over 155,000+ courses in multiple languages on programming, development, IT certifications, Project Management and more.

- Lifetime Access: Once you purchase a course, you have lifetime access to the content.

- Affordable Pricing: Frequent discounts and promotions make courses accessible at lower costs.

- Practical Focus: Many courses are project-based, providing real-world applications.

Popular Courses

- The Complete Python Bootcamp: From Zero to Hero in Python
- AWS Certified Solutions Architect - Associate 2023
- The Complete JavaScript Course 2023: From Zero to Expert

c. **LinkedIn Learning**

Overview

LinkedIn Learning offers a vast library of video courses taught by industry experts in software development, IT, creative, and business skills.

Key Features

- Personalized Recommendations: Course suggestions based on your profile and career interests.

- Certifications: Completion certificates that can be added to your LinkedIn profile.

- Expert Instructors: Courses created and delivered by industry professionals and thought leaders.

- Learning Paths: Structured learning paths to guide you through a series of related courses.

Popular Courses

- Learning Python

- CompTIA A+ (220-1001) Cert Prep

- Learning Cloud Computing: Core Concepts

d. **Pluralsight**

Overview

Pluralsight is a technology-focused platform offering courses and assessments for IT professionals and developers.

Key Features

- Skill Assessments: Skill IQ and Role IQ assessments to measure your proficiency and recommend learning paths.

- Hands-on Labs: Interactive labs and sandbox environments for practical experience.

- Paths and Channels: Curated learning paths and channels to guide your learning journey.

- Certification Prep: Courses designed to prepare you for industry certifications.

Popular Courses

- Python Fundamentals

- AWS Certified Solutions Architect - Associate

- Ethical Hacking: Introduction to Ethical Hacking

e. **edX**

Overview

edX, founded by Harvard and MIT, offers high-quality courses from the world's best universities and institutions.

Key Features

- University-Backed: Courses and programs from top universities like MIT, Harvard, and Berkeley.

- MicroMasters and Professional Certificates: In-depth, career-focused programs that offer a pathway to master's degrees.

- Self-Paced and Scheduled: Flexible options to learn at your own pace or follow a structured schedule.

- Interactive Learning: Includes video lectures, quizzes, and peer discussion forums.

Popular Courses

- CS50's Introduction to Computer Science by Harvard University

- Professional Certificate in Data Science by IBM

- MicroMasters in Cybersecurity by Rochester Institute of Technology

Tips for Leveraging Online Courses and Certifications

a. Set Clear Goals:

- Identify what you want to achieve with your learning. Whether it's mastering a new programming language, earning a certification, or learning a new technology, having clear goals will keep you focused and motivated.

b. Choose the Right Course:

- Research and select courses that align with your career goals and skill level. Read reviews, check the course content, and ensure it covers the topics you need.

c. Create a Learning Schedule:

- Allocate specific times each week for your learning activities. Consistency is key to making steady progress.

d. Engage Actively:

- Participate in discussions, complete assignments, and apply what you learn through projects or hands-on practice.

e. Track Your Progress:

- Use tools like spreadsheets or learning platforms' progress-tracking features to monitor your progress and stay on track with your goals.

f. Apply Your Knowledge:

- Seek opportunities to apply your new skills at work or through personal projects. Practical application reinforces learning and demonstrates your capabilities.

g. Network and Collaborate:

- Join study groups, forums, or online communities related to your courses. Networking with peers can provide additional insights, support, and opportunities for collaboration.

Conclusion

It's essential for IT professionals to leverage online courses and certifications to stay current, advance their careers, and achieve both personal and professional goals. Platforms such as Coursera, Udemy, LinkedIn Learning, Pluralsight, and edX provide a wide range of high-quality courses and certifications specifically designed for aspiring and current IT professionals. By setting clear objectives, selecting the right courses, and actively engaging in the learning process, IT professionals can effectively address skill gaps, enhance their expertise, and remain competitive in the ever-evolving tech industry.

Role of Mentorship and Networking

Engaging with a mentor is a crucial step in your career. A mentor is an experienced professional who can provide guidance and support to help you progress. While this may seem like a simple step, it is often overlooked, even though it plays a significant role in your career journey. We will explore the importance of mentorship and networking.

Importance of Mentorship

a. Guidance and Support:

- Mentors provide valuable guidance and support, helping mentees navigate their career paths, make informed decisions, and overcome challenges.

b. Knowledge Transfer:

- Mentors share their expertise, experience, and industry insights, offering mentees the opportunity to learn from someone who has already walked the path they are aspiring to follow.

c. Skill Development:

- Through regular interactions and feedback, mentors can help mentees develop both technical and soft skills, enhancing their overall competence and confidence.

d. Networking Opportunities:

- Mentors can introduce mentees to their professional network, providing access to new contacts, job opportunities, and industry events.

e. Career Advancement:

- Having a mentor can significantly impact career growth by providing personalized advice, setting career goals, and opening doors to new opportunities.

Importance of Networking

a. Building Relationships:

- Networking helps IT professionals build meaningful relationships with peers, colleagues, industry leaders, and potential employers.

b. Knowledge Sharing:

- Engaging with a professional network facilitates the exchange of ideas, best practices, and emerging trends, keeping you informed and ahead in your field.

c. Career Opportunities:

- A strong network can lead to job referrals, recommendations, and collaborations, which can be crucial for career advancement.

d. Professional Development:

- Networking events, such as conferences and seminars, offer opportunities for learning and development through workshops, keynote speeches, and panel discussions.

e. Support System:

- A robust professional network provides a support system for advice, encouragement, and feedback, which can be invaluable during challenging times in your career.

Pursue and Engage a Mentor

It's very important to find the right mentor. It can make your career, if you align to the right mentor. We shall see how collaboration with mentors can be pursued.

Pursue a Mentor

a. Identify Your Goals:

- Determine what you want to achieve through mentorship. Identify specific skills you want to develop, career goals, or challenges you need help with.

b. Look Within Your Network:

- Start by looking for potential mentors within your current network, such as colleagues, managers, or industry connections who have the expertise and experience relevant to your goals.

c. Professional Associations and Organizations:

- Join professional associations and organizations in your industry. These groups often have mentorship programs or can help you connect with potential mentors.

d. Online Platforms:

- Utilize online platforms like LinkedIn to identify and connect with professionals who inspire you and whose career paths align with your goals. Look for people who share insightful content or have a background in areas you're interested in.

e. Industry Events:

- Attend industry events, conferences, and workshops. These events provide opportunities to meet and interact with experienced professionals who might be willing to mentor you.

f. Mentorship Programs:

- Explore formal mentorship programs offered by your company, industry groups, or educational institutions. These programs often match mentees with mentors based on their goals and interests.

Engaging a Mentor

a. Set Clear Expectations:

- Communicate your goals, expectations, and what you hope to achieve from the mentorship. Discuss the frequency and format of meetings and preferred communication methods.

b. Be Prepared:

- Come to each meeting with a clear agenda, questions, and topics you want to discuss. Being prepared shows respect for your mentor's time and ensures productive sessions.

c. Be Open to Feedback:

- Be receptive to constructive criticism and feedback. Use it as an opportunity to learn and grow, even if it's challenging to hear.

d. Take Initiative:

- Take ownership of your learning and development. Implement your mentor's advice, follow up on action items, and seek additional resources or opportunities to practice what you've learned.

e. Show Appreciation:

- Express gratitude for your mentor's time, guidance, and support. Acknowledge their contributions to your growth and let them know the impact they've made.

f. Reflect and Review:

- Regularly reflect on your progress and the mentorship relationship. Review your goals and adjust them as needed. Discuss the mentorship's effectiveness with your mentor and make changes if necessary.

Building a Strong Networking Strategy

A multi-prong approach can be adopted for having a robust networking strategy.

a. Attend Industry Events:

- Participate in conferences, seminars, webinars, and meetups related to your field. These events provide opportunities to meet new people, learn from industry leaders, and expand your network.

b. Join Professional Organizations:

- Become a member of professional associations and organizations relevant to your career. Engage in their activities, attend events, and participate in online forums and discussions.

c. Leverage Social Media:

- Use platforms like LinkedIn to connect with industry professionals, join groups, participate in discussions, and share valuable content. Build an online presence that reflects your professional interests and expertise.

d. Offer Help and Value:

  • Networking is a two-way street. Offer your assistance, share your knowledge, and provide value to your connections. Building strong relationships often starts with giving before receiving.

e. Follow Up:

  • After meeting some new SMEs, follow up with a personalized message to reinforce the connection. Reference your conversation and express interest in staying in touch. Have a further meeting to discuss/review any relevant topic/event.

f. Stay Informed and Engaged:

  • Keep up with industry news, trends, and developments. Engage in discussions, share relevant content, and stay active in your network to maintain and strengthen your relationships.

Conclusion

For IT professionals, mentorship and networking are essential for career growth and success. Mentorship offers personalized guidance, support, and skill development, while networking creates opportunities for knowledge sharing and professional advancement. By actively seeking mentors and building a strong professional network, IT professionals can enhance their skills, stay informed about industry trends, and navigate their career paths with confidence and support.

Participating in Hackathons and IT Communities

What are Hackathons:

The Hackathons are time-bound events, usually lasting from a day to a week or two, where IT professionals, developers, designers, and other tech enthusiasts come together to collaborate on software projects. The participants typically work in teams to solve specific challenges, build prototypes, or create innovative solutions within the given timeframe. Usually, this is treated as a challenge competition and High Contributors/ Winners are identified at the end of the process.

What are IT Communities:

The IT communities are groups of professionals and enthusiasts who share a common interest in information technology. These communities can be online or offline and focus on various aspects of IT, such as programming languages, cybersecurity, data science, cloud computing, and more. Examples include forums, social media groups, local meetups, and professional associations.

We shall see the benefits of participating in Hackathons and Communities and how to get started with it.

Benefits of Participating in Hackathons

a. Skill Enhancement:

- Hands-On Experience: Hackathons provide an opportunity to apply theoretical knowledge to real-world problems, allowing you to gain practical experience.

- Learning New Technologies: Participants often experiment with new tools, frameworks, and technologies, enhancing their technical skill set.

b. Networking:

- Collaborating with Peers: Working in teams helps you connect with like-minded professionals, fostering collaboration and knowledge exchange.

- Meeting Industry Experts: Many hackathons are sponsored or judged by industry leaders, providing a chance to interact with and learn from experts.

c. Creativity and Innovation:

- Creative Problem-Solving: The competitive and time-bound nature of hackathons encourages innovative thinking and rapid prototyping.

- Exploring New Ideas: Hackathons provide a platform to test and validate new concepts, which can lead to groundbreaking solutions.

d. Career Opportunities:

- Showcasing Skills: Demonstrating your abilities in a hackathon can attract the attention of potential employers or clients.

- Job Offers and Internships: Some companies use hackathons as a recruiting tool, offering job opportunities to standout participants.

e. Teamwork and Leadership:

- Collaborative Skills: Working in a team environment helps improve communication, collaboration, and conflict resolution skills.

- Leadership Opportunities: Leading a team or project within a hackathon can develop and showcase your leadership abilities.

Benefits of Participating in IT Communities

a. Knowledge Sharing:

- Access to Expertise: IT communities are rich with experts willing to share their knowledge, providing answers to questions and solutions to problems.

- Staying Updated: Communities discuss the latest trends, technologies, and best practices, keeping you informed about industry developments.

b. Professional Growth:

- Learning Opportunities: Participating in discussions, attending webinars, and engaging in community events contribute to continuous learning.

- Mentorship and Guidance: Many communities offer mentorship programs, where experienced professionals guide and support less experienced members.

c. Networking:

- Building Connections: Engaging in IT communities helps you build a strong professional network, which can be valuable for career advancement and job searches.

- Collaborative Projects: Communities often collaborate on projects or initiatives, providing opportunities to work with diverse teams.

d. Visibility and Recognition:

- Showcasing Expertise: Sharing your knowledge and contributions can position you as an expert in your field, enhancing your professional reputation.

- Speaking Opportunities: Active community members are often invited to speak at events, write articles, or lead discussions, further increasing their visibility.

e. Support and Motivation:

- Peer Support: Being part of a community provides a support system where members encourage and motivate each other.

- Problem Solving: Communities are excellent resources for troubleshooting and solving technical issues, with collective knowledge and experience at your disposal.

How to Get Started

a. Identify Relevant Hackathons and Communities:

- Hackathons: Look for local, national, or virtual hackathons that match your interests and skills. Websites like Devpost, HackerEarth, and Major League Hacking list upcoming events.

- IT Communities: Join online forums (e.g., Stack Overflow, Reddit), social media groups (e.g., LinkedIn groups, Facebook groups), and local meetups (e.g., Meetup.com).

b. Engage Actively:

- Participate Regularly: Attend events, contribute to discussions, and share your knowledge and experiences.

- Volunteer: Offer to help organize events, mentor new members, or contribute to community projects.

c. Set Goals:

- Personal Development: Define what you want to achieve through participation, such as learning new skills, networking, or finding job opportunities.

- Community Contribution: Aim to contribute value to the community by sharing your expertise, offering help, and promoting collaborative efforts.

d. Leverage Resources:

- Learning Materials: Utilize the resources provided by communities, such as tutorials, webinars, and discussion forums, to enhance your knowledge.

- Networking Opportunities: Take advantage of networking events and platforms to build relationships with other professionals.

Conclusion

Participating in hackathons and IT communities offers numerous benefits for IT professionals, including skill enhancement, networking opportunities, and avenues for career growth. By actively engaging in these activities, IT professionals can stay updated on industry trends, develop new skills, and build valuable connections while contributing to the broader tech and project management community. Hackathons and IT communities create a dynamic and supportive environment that fosters innovation, collaboration, and career advancement. IT professionals should take advantage of these opportunities to maximize their skill development and demonstrate their progress.

Chapter 6

Educational Paths and Certifications

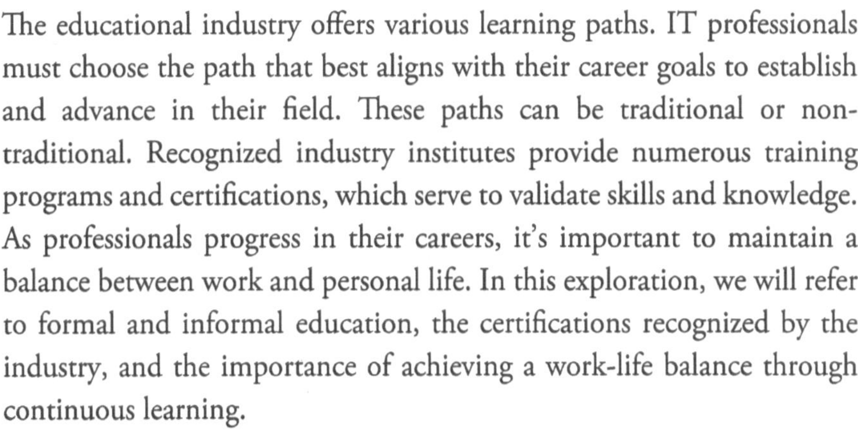

The educational industry offers various learning paths. IT professionals must choose the path that best aligns with their career goals to establish and advance in their field. These paths can be traditional or non-traditional. Recognized industry institutes provide numerous training programs and certifications, which serve to validate skills and knowledge. As professionals progress in their careers, it's important to maintain a balance between work and personal life. In this exploration, we will refer to formal and informal education, the certifications recognized by the industry, and the importance of achieving a work-life balance through continuous learning.

Traditional Educational Paths

1. Bachelor's Degree:

   - Duration: Typically, 3 to 4 years.

   - Curriculum: Comprehensive study including core subjects, electives, and major-specific courses.

   - Benefits: Broad knowledge base, recognized by most employers, access to campus resources, networking opportunities.

- Examples: 3 years of BSc in Computer Science, BSc in Information Technology. Or 4 years of Engineering - BE, BTech

2. Master's Degree:

- Duration: Typically, 2 years.

- Curriculum: Advanced coursework and specialization in specific IT areas.

- Benefits: Deeper expertise, is often required for higher-level positions and research opportunities.

- Examples: MSc in Cybersecurity, MSc in Data Science, ME, MTech in Computer Science

Non-Traditional Educational Paths

1. Institutional Training / Bootcamps:

- Duration: Usually 3-6 months.

- Curriculum: Intensive, focused training on specific skills such as coding, data science, or cybersecurity.

- Benefits: Short duration, hands-on experience, industry-relevant skills, often includes career support with job opportunities search.

- Examples: Language training like Java, C#; Coding boot camps, Data Science boot camps.

2. Self-Learning:

- Duration: Flexible, self-paced.

- Curriculum: Varied, based on individual goals and resources.

- Benefits: Cost-effective, flexible schedule, access to a plethora of free/paid online resources.

- Examples: Online courses (Coursera, edX), tutorials, MOOCs, books, forums.

Certifications in IT

The Certifications play a crucial role in validating skills and knowledge for IT professionals. We will explore some important certifications in key areas for IT Professionals.

a. Programming and Development:

- Oracle Certified Professional Java Programmer (OCJP): Proficiency in Java programming

- Microsoft Certified: Azure Developer Associate: Development on Microsoft Azure.

- Amazon, Google, and IBM have similar Developer and Architect Certifications, for their respective platforms.

b. Software Testing:

- ISTQB® is the leading global certification scheme in the field of software testing.

- Certified Tester Foundation Level (CTFL): Practical knowledge of Software Testing.

- Advanced Agile Technical Tester (CTAL-ATT): A thorough introduction to Agile technical testing.

c. IT Architect:

- Open Group Certified Architect (Open CA): It's a premier, global certification for certifying skills and experience in the IT Architecture community

d. Networking:

- CompTIA Network+: Entry-level certification for networking.

- Cisco Certified Network Associate (CCNA): Fundamental networking skills.

e. Cybersecurity:

- Certified Information Systems Security Professional (CISSP): Advanced security management.

- Certified Ethical Hacker (CEH): Offensive security skills.

f. Cloud Computing:

- Foundation, Associate, Professional - Developer, Solution Architect Certifications in AWS, Azure, Google, IBM Cloud Platforms

g. Data Science & Analytics:

- Certified Data Professional (CDP): Broad-based data skills.

- Google Data Analytics Professional Certificate: Practical data analysis skills.

h. Project Management:

- PMI Project Management Professional (PMP): Comprehensive project management skills.

- PMI Program Management Professional (PgMP): Program management skills.

- ITIL: best practices for IT service management (ITSM) to support the standardisation of various processes and stages in the IT lifecycle.

- Edureka's PRINCE2: The Foundation and Practitioner course will help you understand various concepts like the PRINCE2 process, principles, and methods for the Project Manager, Project Coordinator, and Program Manager roles.

i. Agile Certifications:

- Certified Scrum Master (CSM): Agile project management with Scrum.

- Certified Scrum Product Owner (CSPO): validate Agile Product Owner process knowledge.

- PMI Agile Certified Practitioner (ACP) - validates your ability to drive excellence across Methodologies, with Agile Ceremonies.

- PMI Disciplined Agile Senior Scrum Master (DASSM) – validate the use of the Disciplined Agile (DA™) tool kit to optimize teams' work

Conclusion

IT professionals can choose the right educational path and certifications based on their individual aspirations, goals, time, resources, and the specific IT domain they wish to pursue. A blend of traditional education, boot camps, self-learning, and relevant certifications can create a strong foundation for a successful career in IT.

The Value of Higher Education in IT

Higher education in Information Technology (IT) encompasses formal degrees such as Bachelor's, Master's, and Ph.D. programs. These programs are offered by universities and colleges and provide a structured, comprehensive approach to learning. We shall see the benefits and limitations of formal education.

Benefits of Formal Education in IT

a. Structured Learning Path:

- Comprehensive Curriculum: A degree program covers a wide range of topics, including fundamental concepts, advanced theories, and practical applications.

- Sequenced Courses: Courses are arranged logically, ensuring a progressive build-up of knowledge.

b. Accreditation and Recognition:

- Widely Recognized Credentials: Degrees from accredited institutions are globally recognized and often preferred by employers.

- Standardized Quality: Accreditation ensures that the education provided meets specific quality standards.

c. Access to Resources:

- State-of-the-Art Facilities: Universities often provide access to advanced labs, research facilities, and technology.

- Library and Online Resources: Students have access to extensive academic libraries and online journals.

d. Networking Opportunities:

- Alumni Networks: Graduates can connect with alumni, providing valuable networking opportunities for job placements and career advancement.

- Industry Connections: Universities often have partnerships with tech companies, offering internships and job placements.

e. All Round Development:

- Soft Skills Training: In addition to technical skills, formal education emphasizes the development of communication, public speaking, teamwork, and problem-solving skills.

- Extracurricular Activities: Opportunities to participate in competitions, social services, and events that enhance personal and professional growth.

f. Research Opportunities:

- Innovation and Development: Universities provide a platform for research, encouraging students to innovate and contribute to the field.

- Graduate Studies: Opportunities for advanced research and specialization through Master's and Ph.D. programs.

Some Organizations offer higher education support when you are employed for a job. For the distance learning program, the job could be continued; for the full-time course, the employment could be retained, at the discretion of the organization.

Limitations of Formal Education in IT

a. Cost:

- High Tuition Fees: The cost of a degree can be substantial, including tuition, books, and living expenses.

- Student Debt: Many students incur significant debt to finance their education.

b. Time Commitment:

- Duration: Bachelor's programs typically take 4 years, and Master's programs take an additional 1 2 years.

- Full-Time Commitment: Most degree programs require full-time study, limiting the ability to work concurrently.

c. Rapidly Changing Technology:

- Outdated Curriculum: The fast pace of technological advancement can render some aspects of the curriculum outdated by the time students graduate.

- Need for Continuous Learning: Graduates must continue learning and updating their skills even after completing their degree.

d. Limited Practical Experience:

- Theory-Heavy: Some programs may focus more on theoretical knowledge than practical, hands-on experience.

- Lack of Industry Exposure: Limited real-world exposure can be a disadvantage compared to alternative education paths like boot camps or apprenticeships. A Sandwich course, with a combination of Industry experience for about 1-2 terms can be opted, for from a good University/Institute.

e. Variable Quality:

- Institutional Differences: The quality of education can vary significantly between institutions.

- Dependence on Faculty: The effectiveness of the education often depends on the quality and dedication of the faculty.

Conclusion

Higher education in IT offers a strong foundation, recognized credentials, and access to a wide range of resources and opportunities. However, it also involves significant costs, time commitments, and the necessity for continuous skill updates due to the fast-paced evolution of technology. To maximize their potential and remain relevant in the industry, IT professionals should balance formal education with ongoing self-learning, certifications, and practical experience.

Industry-recognised certifications and Their Benefits

Industry-recognized certifications are credentials awarded to professionals who pass exams that validate their expertise in specific areas of IT. These certifications are highly regarded by employers and can significantly enhance a professional's career prospects.

Benefits of Industry-Recognized Certifications

a. Career Advancement:

- Promotion Opportunities: Certifications can lead to higher opportunities and positions with increased responsibilities.

- Salary Increases: Certified professionals often command more opportunities and in turn, higher salaries than their non-certified peers.

b. Skill Validation:

- Credibility: Certifications provide renowned third-party validation of a professional's skills and knowledge.

- Up-to-date Knowledge: They ensure that professionals stay current with the latest technologies and best practices.

c. Competitive Advantage:

- Job Market: Certified professionals have an edge in a competitive job market.

- Differentiation: Certifications help differentiate candidates at the selection by employers.

d. Networking Opportunities:

- Professional Communities: Certification programs often include access to exclusive professional networks and communities.

- Industry Connections: Opportunities to connect with peers, mentors, and industry leaders.

e. Personal Development:

- Continual Learning: Preparing for certifications encourages continuous learning and professional growth.

- Confidence: Earning certifications boosts confidence for the individual.

Key Certifications for IT Professionals

We will consider the important certifications for various IT roles, providers, focus areas and benefits.

- Project Management Professional (PMP):

  - Provider: Project Management Institute (PMI)

  - Focus: Project management principles and methodologies.

  - Benefits:

    - Recognized globally as the very high standard in worldwide project management.

    - Validates skills in leading and directing projects.

    - Increases job prospects in a variety of industries.

- AWS Certified Solutions Architect:

  - Provider: Amazon Web Services (AWS)

  - Focus: Designing and deploying scalable systems on the AWS Cloud platform.

  - Benefits:

    - Demonstrates proficiency in AWS technologies.

    - Enhances career opportunities in cloud computing.

    - Highly sought after by employers using AWS services.

- Certified Information Systems Security Professional (CISSP):

  - Provider: (ISC)^2

  - Focus: Information security and risk management.

  - Benefits:

    - Recognized as a premier certifiction in cybersecurity.

    - Validate ability to design, implement, and manage a best-in-class cybersecurity program.

    - Required for many high-level security positions.

- Certified Ethical Hacker (CEH):
  - Provider: EC-Council
  - Focus: Ethical hacking and penetration testing.
  - Benefits:
    - Validates skills in identifying and addressing security vulnerabilities.
    - Increases opportunities in cybersecurity roles.
    - Recognized by employers and government agencies.
- CompTIA Network+:
  - Provider: CompTIA
  - Focus: Foundational networking concepts and skills.
  - Benefits:
    - Ideal for entry-level network professionals.
    - Provides a strong foundation for advanced networking certifications.
    - Recognized by employers worldwide.
- Microsoft Certified: Azure Solutions Architect Expert:
  - Provider: Microsoft
  - Focus: Designing and implementing solutions on Microsoft Azure.
  - Benefits:
    - Demonstrates expertise in Microsoft Azure.
    - Enhances career prospects in cloud architecture.
    - Sought after by employers using Microsoft Azure.

- Google Professional Data Engineer:
  - Provider: Google Cloud
  - Focus: Designing and building data processing systems on Google Cloud Platform (GCP).
  - Benefits:
    - Validates skills in data engineering and GCP technologies.
    - Improves job prospects in data engineering roles.
    - Recognized by employers using GCP.
- Cisco Certified Network Associate (CCNA)
  - Provider: Cisco
  - Focus: Networking fundamentals, including routing and switching.
  - Benefits:
    - Establishes a strong foundation in networking.
    - Prerequisite for advanced Cisco certifications.
    - Highly regarded by employers in networking roles.

Conclusion

Certifications are essential for reinforcing your skills, validating them with third-party vendors, and showcasing your capabilities and achievements to your organization. They boost your confidence in the industry and the job market. Industry-recognized certifications hold significant value and are particularly important for IT professionals who want to validate their skills and advance their careers. They help you stay updated with the latest technology trends.

In addition to personal development, certifications offer various benefits, including career advancement, skill validation, a competitive advantage, and networking opportunities. Key certifications such as PMI PMP, ACP, DASSM, AWS Certified Solutions Architect, CISSP, CEH, CompTIA Network+, Microsoft Azure Solutions Architect Expert, Google Professional Data Engineer, and CCNA are highly respected in the industry. Earning these certifications can significantly enhance your career prospects as an IT professional.

Balancing Work, Life, and Continuous Learning

The work-life balance and consistent learning are crucial for IT professionals to maintain productivity, personal welfare, and career growth. The fast-paced nature of the IT industry demands constant skill updates while managing professional commitments, and personal responsibilities. We shall see the importance and time management for the work-life balance.

Importance of Balance in Personal Life

a. Avoiding Burnout:

- Mental Health: Continuous high stress levels can lead to burnout, affecting mental health.

- Sustained Productivity: Proper balance helps in maintaining long-term productivity.

b. Career Growth:

- Skill Enhancement: Continuous learning is essential for staying relevant and advancing in the career.

- Innovation and Creativity: A well-balanced life fosters creativity and innovative thinking.

c. Personal Fulfilment:

- Quality Time: Spending time with family and friends is crucial for personal happiness.

- Hobbies and Interests: Pursuing personal interests can lead to a more fulfilled life.

Time Management Tips for IT Professionals

Time is money, and it's very important to manage it well. See how to do it and follow.

a. Prioritize Tasks

One should study the well-known Eisenhower Matrix to Categorize tasks into four quadrants:

1. Urgent and Important

2. Important but Not Urgent

3. Urgent but Not Important

4. Not Urgent and Not Important

- Always Focus on High-Impact Tasks: Prioritize tasks that significantly impact your goals and responsibilities.

You would carry an exercise to list down all the ToDo's on a Day / Week / Month basis, categorize them into the 4 quadrants of the Eisenhower matrix, and act as advised for each category. This will considerably improve your time management and speed up your work execution.

➤ Task Prioritization with the Eisenhower matrix – refer to Annexure B-4

b. Set Clear Goals:

- SMART Goals: Set Specific, Measurable, Achievable, Relevant, and Time-bound goals for both work and learning.

- Daily and Weekly Planning: Break down larger goals into manageable daily and weekly tasks.

c. Create a Schedule:

- Dedicated Learning Time: Allocate specific time slots for learning new skills or studying for certifications.

- Work-Life Boundaries: Set clear boundaries between work hours and personal time to avoid overlap.

d. Utilize Technology:

- Productivity Tools: Use tools like Trello, Asana, or Microsoft ToDo for task management.

- Learning Platforms: Leverage online learning platforms such as Coursera, Udemy, and Pluralsight for flexible learning schedules.

e. Practice Time Blocking:

- Block Time for Specific Tasks: Allocate dedicated blocks of time for focused work, learning, and personal activities.

- Minimize Interruptions: Use time blocks to minimize distractions and improve concentration.

f. Take Breaks:

- Pomodoro Technique: Work in 25-minute intervals followed by a 5-minute break. Take a longer break after four intervals.

- Regular Breaks: Short breaks during work hours help maintain energy levels and productivity.

g. Learn to Say No:

This is a very important trait one should have. By nature and cultural impact, mostly, saying No is not opted due to shyness or other person's personality impact.

- Avoid Overcommitment: Politely decline additional tasks or projects that may overwhelm your schedule.

- Delegate Tasks: Delegate tasks, when possible, to manage workload effectively.

h. Leverage Downtime:

- Microlearning: Utilize short periods of downtime (e.g., commuting, waiting) for microlearning sessions.

- Podcasts and Audiobooks: Listen to industry-related podcasts or audiobooks during commutes or while exercising.

i. Maintain Physical Health:

- Regular Exercise: Incorporate regular physical activity to reduce stress and increase energy levels. Always ensure to remain fit for the ever-demanding Industry job and responsibilities.

- Healthy Eating: Maintain a balanced diet to ensure sustained energy and focus.

j. Seek Support:

- Mentorship: Seek guidance from mentors or colleagues to manage career growth and continuous learning.

- Professional Communities: Join professional communities or groups for support, networking, and shared learning.

Conclusion

Achieving work-life balance and ongoing learning requires careful planning and effective time management. IT professionals can create a healthy balance that promotes both professional success and personal well-being by prioritizing their work, setting clear goals, organizing a structured schedule, and making the most of technology.

To attain work-life balance, it's essential to plan time wisely, take regular breaks, learn to say no (which is very important), utilize downtime effectively, maintain physical health, and seek support when needed. Once this crucial balance is achieved, significant growth for IT professionals becomes much more attainable.

Chapter 7

Role of Experience in Career Growth

Gaining industrial work experience involves spending time in a company setting where you acquire new skills and gain practical knowledge. Such experiences provide insights into essential skills, the work environment, and the key responsibilities associated with a particular profession. This understanding enables you to identify ways to improve and focus your future efforts. Industrial work experience is crucial for your career growth.

We will explore the significance of work experience and the various ways it can be pursued. Additionally, we will examine how to effectively showcase this experience on your resume, and if you encounter setbacks, how to transform those challenges into opportunities for success. We will also share a success story to illustrate these points.

Importance of Experience

a. Practical Knowledge:

- Application of Theory: Experience allows IT professionals to apply theoretical knowledge to real-world situations, enhancing their understanding and problem-solving skills.

- Skill Development: Hands-on experience helps develop and refine technical and soft skills, making professionals more effective in their roles.

b. Career Advancement:

- Increased Employability: Employers value candidates with relevant experience, making it easier to secure job offers and promotions.

- Professional Growth: Experience provides a foundation for continuous learning and skill enhancement, leading to career progression.

c. Networking:

- Industry Connections: Working on projects and internships helps build a network of industry contacts, which can be valuable for future job opportunities and collaborations.

- Mentorship: The experienced senior colleagues can provide guidance and mentorship, aiding in career development for the individuals.

d. Confidence Building:

- Competence: Gaining experience in technology and management areas, boosts confidence in the professional's abilities to handle complex delivery, risks and challenges within it.

- Leadership: Experience in various roles can enhance the capabilities of IT professionals for leadership and management positions in the higher ladder of the management chain.

Relevant Experience through Internships and Projects

We shall explore how the experience can be pursued with internships and projects, that you can account as valid experience in the CV and interviews.

Internships

a. Introduction to the Industry:

- Real-World Exposure: Internships offer a glimpse into the daily operations and challenges of the IT industry.

- Learning Environment: Interns are often given opportunities to learn and experiment without the high stakes of full-time positions.

b. Application of Skills:

- Hands-On Tasks: Internships provide practical tasks that help interns apply their academic knowledge.

- Problem-solving: Real-world problems enhance analytical and problem-solving skills.

c. Professional Development:

- Workplace Etiquette: Interns learn professional behaviour, communication, and collaboration.

- Feedback: Constructive feedback from supervisors helps improve performance and skills.

d. Resume Creation:

- Experience: Internships add valuable experience to resumes, making candidates more attractive to employers.

- References: Supervisors and colleagues can provide references for future job applications.

Projects

a. Portfolio Creation:

- Showcase Skills: Personal or collaborative projects can be showcased in portfolios to demonstrate skills to potential employers.

- Diverse Experience: Projects can cover various aspects of IT, such as development, cybersecurity, data analysis, and more.

b. Learning and Experimentation:

- Skill Enhancement: Projects provide opportunities to learn new technologies and methodologies.

- Innovation: Working on unique projects encourages innovative thinking and creativity.

c. Team Collaboration:

- Group Projects: Collaborating on projects with peers simulates real-world team dynamics and improves teamwork skills.

- Open-Source Contributions: Contributing to open-source projects can provide experience and recognition within the tech community.

Finding and Applying for Internships

Now we will see how to find Internship opportunities and pursue them.

➤ Finding Internships

a. Online Job Portals:

- Dedicated Platforms: Websites like Indeed, Glassdoor, LinkedIn, and Internshala specialize in listing internship opportunities.

- Company Websites: Many companies post internship openings on their career pages.

b. University Career Centres:

- Job Fairs: Attend career fairs and networking events organized by universities.

- Advisors: Career advisors can provide leads and guidance on finding internships.

c. Professional Networks:

- LinkedIn: Use LinkedIn to connect with industry professionals and join relevant groups.

- Networking Events: Attend industry conferences, meetups, and seminars to network with potential employers.

d. Online Communities:

- Forums and Groups: Participate in online forums and groups like Reddit, GitHub, and Stack Overflow, where internship opportunities are often shared.

- Social media: Follow companies and industry leaders on social media platforms for updates on internship openings.

➤ Applying for Internships

a. Tailored Resumes and Cover Letters:

- Customize: Tailor your resume and cover letter for each internship application, highlighting relevant skills and experiences.

- Keywords: Use keywords from the job description to pass through Applicant Tracking Systems (ATS).

b. Portfolio:

- Showcase Projects: Include a link to an online portfolio or GitHub repository showcasing your projects and skills.

- Documentation: Provide clear documentation and descriptions of your projects.

c. Professional Communication:

- Formal Email: Write a formal email when applying, addressing the hiring manager and expressing your enthusiasm for the position.

- Follow-up: Send a polite follow-up email if you haven't heard back within a couple of weeks.

    d. Interview Preparation:

- Research: Research the company and the role thoroughly before the interview.

- Practice: Prepare for common technical and behavioural interview questions.

    e. Leverage Referrals:

- Connections: If you know someone at the company, ask for a referral as it can increase your chances of getting noticed.

Conclusion

For IT professionals, advancing in their careers requires gaining relevant experience through internships and projects. Internships provide practical exposure, allow for the application of skills, and contribute to professional development. On the other hand, projects present opportunities for innovation and help in building a strong portfolio.

To find and apply for internships, it is helpful to utilize online platforms, university resources, and professional networks, along with effective application strategies. Balancing work, life, and continuous learning, while acquiring relevant experience, is essential for sustained career growth and personal fulfilment in the IT industry.

Hands-On Practice and Real-World Application

The theoretical knowledge gained in education does not necessarily help in industrial work. For that actual work experience, exposure to various situations and tools/techniques is very much required. We will see the importance of it.

Importance of Hands-On Practice and Real-World Application

a. Enhanced Learning and Retention:

- Active Engagement: The practical work involves active engagement, with hands-on work, decision-making, risks and issues identification and mitigation. This significantly improves understanding and retention compared to passive learning.

- Immediate Feedback: The Real-world application provides immediate feedback, allowing for quick identification and correction of mistakes.

b. Skill Proficiency:

- Practical Skills: Hands-on practice helps in developing practical skills that are directly applicable to job tasks.

- Problem-Solving: Working on real-world problems enhances analytical and problem-solving skills, making professionals more adept at handling challenges.

c. Industry Relevance:

- Current Technologies: Practical work ensures familiarity with current tools, technologies, and practices used in the industry.

- Adaptability: It fosters adaptability, preparing professionals to quickly learn and integrate new technologies as they emerge.

d. Confidence Building:

- Competence: Regular practice builds competence, boosting confidence in one's ability to perform tasks effectively.

- Professional Growth: Confidence gained through hands-on practice translates to better performance and career growth.

e. Portfolio Development:

- Showcase Abilities: Projects and practical work create tangible evidence of skills and knowledge, which can be showcased to potential employers.

- Differentiation: A strong portfolio sets candidates apart in a competitive job market.

Building and Showcasing Individual Projects

We would see how stretch projects can be pursued to develop skills and display them to relevant stakeholders.

➤ Steps to Build Individual Projects

a. Identify Areas of Interest:

- Passion Projects: Choose projects that align with personal interests and career goals to maintain motivation.

- Market Demand: Consider the current demands and trends in the industry to ensure the project is relevant.

b. Define Objectives:

- Clear Goals: Set specific, measurable, achievable, relevant, and time-bound (SMART) goals for the project.

- Scope: Clearly define the scope to avoid project creep and ensure timely completion.

c. Plan and Research:

- Blueprint: Create a detailed plan outlining the steps, resources, and timeline needed for the project.

- Research: Conduct thorough research to understand the requirements, tools, and technologies involved.

d. Choose the Right Tools and Technologies:

- Relevance: Select tools and technologies that are relevant to the project and the industry.

- Accessibility: Ensure the chosen tools are accessible and you have the necessary skills or resources to learn them.

e. Development and Implementation:

- Iterative Process: Develop the project iteratively, testing and refining at each stage.

- Documentation: Maintain clear and detailed documentation of the project, including code comments, design decisions, and problem-solving steps.

f. Testing and Debugging:

- Comprehensive Testing: Test the project thoroughly to identify and fix bugs and ensure functionality.

- User Feedback: If possible, get feedback from potential users or peers to improve the project.

g. Deployment:

- Live Environment: Deploy the project in a live environment if applicable, to showcase its real-world application.

- Maintenance: Regularly update and maintain the project to keep it functional and relevant.

➤ Showcasing Individual Projects

a. Create a Portfolio Website:

- Centralized Platform: Use a personal website to centralize all projects, making it easy for potential employers to view.

- Professional Presentation: Ensure the website is professionally designed and easy to navigate.

b. Use GitHub:

- Public Repositories: Host project code in public repositories on GitHub to showcase coding skills and collaboration.

- Documentation: Include detailed README files and project documentation to explain the purpose, features, and usage of each project.

c. Write Blog Posts:

- Project Insights: Write blog posts detailing the project development process, challenges faced, and solutions implemented.

- SEO Benefits: Regular blogging can improve online visibility and establish you as a knowledgeable professional in your field.

d. Social Media and Professional Networks:

- LinkedIn Share project updates and outcomes on LinkedIn to reach potential employers and industry peers.

- Twitter and Reddit: Use platforms like Twitter and Reddit to engage with the tech community and showcase projects.

e. Networking Events and Meetups:

- Presentations: Present your projects at industry conferences, meetups, and hackathons.

- Demos: Offer to demo your projects in relevant forums to gather feedback and increase visibility.

f. Online Portfolios:

- Portfolio Platforms: Use platforms like Behance or Dribbble for design-related projects, or Kaggle for data science projects.

- Showcase Platforms: Participate in online showcases or competitions to gain recognition.

Conclusion

Practical experience and real-world applications are essential for IT professionals to develop valuable skills, maintain industry relevance, and build confidence. Creating and showcasing personal projects not only enhances learning and retention but also results in a tangible portfolio that demonstrates skills to potential employers. By following organized steps to build these projects and presenting them effectively, IT professionals can greatly improve their career prospects and professional growth.

Building a Strong Professional Portfolio

A strong professional portfolio is essential for showcasing your skills, experiences, and projects to potential employers. It serves as tangible evidence of your abilities and helps you stand out in the competitive job market.

Key Components of a Professional Portfolio

a. Personal Information:

- Professional Summary: A brief overview of your background, skills, and career goals.

- Contact Information: Email address, LinkedIn profile, and other relevant contact details.

b. Resume/CV:

- Detailed Experience: Include your professional experience, education, certifications, and relevant Skills.

- Tailored Content: Customize your resume to highlight experiences and skills relevant to the job you're applying for.

➤ **CV Template – refer to Annexure B-5**

> A bit of explanation on Resume v/s CV…
>
> A CV is a more detailed document that shows your academic and professional attainments. It's often used for positions that require specific knowledge or expertise. A CV can include personal information, for example, degrees, awards, publications etc.
>
> A Resume is a very concise document that marks your most relevant skills, achievements, and experiences for a specific job or career. It's typically one to two pages long and focuses primarily on your work experience.

c. Projects:

- Diverse Selection: Include a variety of projects that demonstrate different skills and technologies.

- Detailed Descriptions: Provide clear descriptions of each project, including your role, the technologies used, and the outcomes achieved.

- Source Code: If possible, include links to the project's source code, hosted on platforms like GitHub.

d. Skills:

- Technical Skills: List programming languages, tools, frameworks, and technologies you are proficient in.

- Soft Skills: Highlight soft skills such as teamwork, communication, problem-solving, and leadership.

e. Certifications and Awards:

- Industry Certifications: Include any relevant industry certifications, such as AWS Certified, PMP, or CISSP.

- Recognition: Mention any awards or recognition received for your work or projects.

f. Testimonials and References:

- Client Feedback: Include testimonials from clients or colleagues that speak to your skills and work ethic.

- Professional References: Provide contact information for references who can vouch for your abilities.

g. Blog/Articles:

- Thought Leadership: Include links to any blog posts or articles you've written on industry topics.

- Showcase Knowledge: Writing about your experiences and insights can demonstrate your expertise and thought leadership.

h. Portfolio Website:

- Professional Presentation: Create a personal website to serve as a centralized hub for all portfolio Components.

- User-Friendly: Ensure the website is easy to navigate, visually appealing, and mobile-friendly.

Establish an Impressive GitHub Profile

A well-maintained GitHub profile is a powerful tool for demonstrating your development and leadership skills and project contributions to prospective employers. It's a way to establish yourself.

- Steps to Create an Impressive GitHub Profile

  a. Complete Your Profile:

    - Profile Picture: Use a professional-looking profile picture.

    - Bio: Write a concise bio that summarizes your professional background and interests.

    - Contact Information: Include links to your portfolio website, LinkedIn profile, and other relevant contact information.

b. Organize Repositories:

- Pinned Repositories: Pin your best and most relevant repositories to the top of your profile to highlight your key projects.

- Descriptive Names: Give repositories clear and descriptive names to make it easy for others to understand their purpose.

c. Detailed README Files:

- Project Overview: Provide a detailed overview of each project, including its purpose, features, and usage instructions.

- Installation and Usage: Include step-by-step instructions for installing and using the project.

- Technologies Used: List the technologies and tools used in the project.

- Screenshots/Demos: Add screenshots or demo links to give a visual overview of the project.

d. Consistent Contributions:

- Regular Commits: Make regular commitments to show consistent activity and engagement.

- Contribution Graph: Maintain a healthy contribution graph by contributing to your own and others' projects regularly.

e. Open-Source Contributions:

- Collaborate on Projects: Contribute to open-source projects to demonstrate collaboration and community involvement.

- Pull Requests: Make meaningful pull requests to other repositories to show your willingness to contribute and improve existing projects.

f. Issue Tracking:

- Report Issues: Actively report and fix issues in your projects and those you contribute to.

- Discussion Participation: Engage in discussions on issues and pull requests to demonstrate your collaborative skills.

g. Documentation:

- Comprehensive Docs: Provide comprehensive documentation for your projects to help others understand and use your work.

- Wiki Pages: Use GitHub's wiki feature for more detailed documentation and guides.

h. Project Boards:

- Task Management: Use GitHub Project Boards to organize tasks, plan project development, and showcase your project management skills.

- Kanban Boards: Implement Kanban boards to visually manage your workflow and demonstrate your organizational abilities.

i. Tags and Releases:

- Versioning: Use tags and releases to mark significant milestones and stable versions of your projects.

- Release Notes: Include detailed release notes to explain new features, fixes, and improvements.

j. Community Engagement:

- Stars and Forks: Star and fork repositories of interest to show your engagement with the community.

- Watch Repositories: Watch repositories to stay updated on projects you're interested in or contributing to.

Conclusion

IT professionals looking to showcase their skills and experiences should focus on building a strong professional portfolio and creating an impressive GitHub profile. A comprehensive portfolio presents your expertise, projects, and achievements, while a well-maintained GitHub profile highlights your coding abilities, project contributions, and engagement with the community. By following these steps, IT professionals can create a compelling representation of their capabilities, thereby enhancing their prospects in the competitive job market.

Lessons from Failures and Iteration to Success

Failures should be viewed as stepping stones to success. We must learn from every failure, big or small, and take proactive corrective actions to safeguard ourselves and ensure continued progress.

Bill Gates, Co-founder of Microsoft has profound comments on the Failure. He said, "It's fine to celebrate success, but it is more important to heed the lessons of failure."

We shall see how failure should be acknowledged and converted to opportunity.

Role of Failure in Professional Growth

a. Valuable Learning Opportunities:

- Insight into Weaknesses: Failures reveal areas that need improvement, providing a clear path for skill enhancement.

- Problem-solving skills: Analysing and understanding failures enhance problem-solving abilities and critical thinking.

b. Innovation and Creativity:

- Encourages Experimentation: Accepting the possibility of failure encourages innovative thinking and experimentation.

- Adaptability: Learning to adapt and pivot from failed attempts fosters creativity and resilience.

c. Building Resilience:

- Mental Fortitude: Overcoming failures builds mental strength and perseverance.

- Long-Term Success: Resilience developed through handling failures contributes to sustained long-term success.

Embracing and Overcoming Failures

With a calculated risk, the failures can be converted into stepping stones for success. We should evaluate it well, to take further steps.

Steps to Embrace and Learn from Failures

a. Acknowledge the Failure:

- Acceptance: Accept that failure is a natural part of the learning process.

- Ownership: Take responsibility for the failure without assigning blame to others.

b. Analyse the Failure:

- Root Cause Analysis: Identify the root causes of the failure by breaking down what went wrong.

- Gather Feedback: Seek feedback from colleagues, mentors, or clients to gain different perspectives.

c. Learn and Document Lessons:

- Identify Lessons Learned: Document the lessons learned from the failure to avoid repeating the same mistakes.

- Knowledge Sharing: Share your experiences and lessons learned with your team or professional community.

d. Develop a Plan for Improvement:

- Actionable Steps: Create a plan with actionable steps to address the identified weaknesses.

- Continuous Improvement: Integrate these steps into your routine to continuously improve and refine your skills.

e. Implement Changes and Iterate:

- Try New Approaches: Apply the lessons learned by experimenting with new approaches and techniques.

- Iterate and Test: Continuously iterate on your solutions, testing and refining them based on the feedback and results.

f. Maintain a Positive Mindset:

- Stay Optimistic: Keep a positive attitude towards failure, viewing it as a learning opportunity rather than a setback.

- Motivation: Use the lessons from failures as motivation to strive for success.

Overcoming Failures in Specific Scenarios

a. Project Failures:

- Root Cause Analysis (RCA): Conduct a thorough post-mortem analysis to understand what went wrong in the project.

- Stakeholder Communication: Communicate transparently with stakeholders about the failure and the steps being taken to address it.

b. Technical Failures:

- Debugging and Testing: Invest time in thorough debugging and testing to identify and fix issues.

- Peer Reviews: Utilize code reviews and peer feedback to catch potential problems early.

c. Career Setbacks:

- Skill Development: Use career setbacks as an opportunity to upskill or reskill in relevant areas.

- Networking: Expand your professional network to find new opportunities and gain support.

Practical Examples of Learning from Failures

We shall explore some live examples of project failures and the RCA and Actions to be taken.

Example 1: Failed Software Deployment

a. Scenario:

- A software deployment caused major system outages and user complaints.

b. Analysis and Learning:

- Root Cause: Insufficient testing and inadequate rollback procedures.

- Lessons Learned: Implement a more rigorous testing protocol and establish clear rollback procedures.

c. Action Plan:

- Develop automated tests and conduct thorough testing in a staging environment.

- Train the team on new deployment and rollback procedures.

Example 2: Unsuccessful Job Application

a. Scenario:

- A job application for a desired position was rejected.

b. Analysis and Learning:

- Root Cause: Lack of certain skills or insufficient interview preparation.

- Lessons Learned: Identify the skills gap and improve interview techniques.

c. Action Plan:

- Take relevant courses or certifications to acquire the necessary skills.

- Practice mock interviews and seek feedback from peers or mentors.

Example 3: Incomplete Project Delivery

a. Scenario:

- A project was delivered late and did not meet all client requirements.

b. Analysis and Learning:

- Root Cause: Poor project planning and scope creep.

- Lessons Learned: Improve project management skills and clearly define project scope from the start.

c. Action Plan:

- Use project management tools to plan and track project progress.

- Establish clear communication channels with clients to manage expectations and scope changes.

Success Story of Jan Koum, co-founder of WhatsApp

Jan Koum, co-founder of WhatsApp, faced numerous challenges early in his career, including rejections from several tech companies. Undeterred, he partnered with Brian Acton to create WhatsApp, which initially struggled to monetize its service.

Despite multifold obstacles, Koum focused on providing a simple, reliable messaging app. WhatsApp's popularity soared, leading to its acquisition by Facebook for US$19 billion in 2014. Koum's journey from immigrant hardships to co-founding one of the most widely used messaging platforms underscores the power of perseverance and a clear vision in overcoming early failures.

Conclusion

For IT professionals to grow and succeed in their careers, it is essential to embrace challenges and learn from failures. By acknowledging setbacks, analysing their causes, and documenting the lessons learned, professionals can update their individual development plans with actionable improvements. Implementing these changes through consistent iteration, while maintaining a positive mindset, fosters resilience and contributes to long-term success. Practical examples demonstrate how learning from failures can lead to significant growth and career advancement for IT professionals.

Navigating Career Change

In many instances throughout an IT career, it may be necessary to change career paths. This could be driven by personal aspirations or shifting business needs. Transitioning from one career path to another often presents challenges, so it is important to plan the change carefully to avoid any negative impact on career progression. In this discussion, we will explore how to transition into key-value roles by taking strategic steps that align our skills and experience with the expectations of those roles.

Strategies for Changing IT Specializations

The field of Information Technology (IT) is vast and dynamic, and technological innovations are happening every day at a rapid pace. The IT Professional is required to adapt to the Changes and keep himself relevant and at par with the industry standards. We would explore the strategies and possible plan steps for IT professionals, considering such a career in terms of role and skill switch.

Understanding the Transition from Developer to Data Scientist

One of the noteworthy transitions in the IT industry is transitioning from a role such as a Developer to a Data Scientist. We will see what possible plan steps and challenges could be.

- Intersection of Skills: Both roles require a strong foundation in analytical skills, programming, and problem-solving.

- Skill Variance: The Developer would have a more granular approach for the application and development of the concerned tech stack following the SDLC cycle, while the Data Scientist would have a higher view of data analysis, statistical modelling, and machine learning. He will have deeper analytical skills and an understanding of the system.

Strategies for a Successful Transition

a. Assess Current Skills and the skill gaps:

  - Self-Evaluation: Assess your current skills in programming languages (e.g., Python, R), data modelling, algorithms, and databases.

  - Identify Skill Gaps: Determine the areas where you need improvement, such as analytical skills, statistical data processing, machine learning techniques, or data visualization tools.

b. Adopt Required Skills and Knowledge:

  - Relevant Education: Explore relevant degree programs or certification courses in Data Science and related fields.

  - Online Courses and Tutorials: Utilize Organizational learnings, or platforms such as Udemy, and Coursera, to learn Data Science, machine learning, and advanced statistical methods.

  - The Certificates like IBM Data Science Professional Certificate or Google Data Analytics can be achieved to strengthen your CV.

c. Achieve Practical Experience:

  - Hands-On Projects: Actual Project work experience is very important. Engage in stretch assignments at your organization, or open-source projects that involve data cleaning, analysis, and modelling.

- Participate in Online Competitions: Join platforms like Kaggle to compete in Data Science challenges and build real-life scenario pilot or POC projects.

- Internships and Part-Time Roles: Look for internships or part-time stretch positions that allow you to work on Data Science projects and gain the required experience.

d. Leverage Your Existing Network:

- Networking: Connect with professionals already in the Data Science field through organisation-level meetings, training, LinkedIn, industry meetups, or professional associations.

- Engage with Mentor: Seek a mentorship from senior experienced Data Scientists, who can help your career aspirations with guidance and insights.

e. Update Your Resume and Online Profiles:

- CV update: Customize your CV to highlight Data Science projects, relevant coursework, and new certifications in Data Science.

- Online Profiles: Update your LinkedIn profile and other professional networks to reflect your skill transition.

f. Preparation for Interviews:

- Technical Interviews: Remain ready for questions related to data manipulation, statistical analysis, and machine learning algorithms. Prepare well for any interview.

- Project Discussions: Rehearse to discuss your Data Science projects in detail, explaining your approach, methodologies, and results.

Additional Resources:

- Books: "Python for Data Analysis" by Wes McKinney, "Data Science from Scratch" by Joel Grus.

- Blogs and Forums: Follow blogs like Towards Data Science and participate in forums like Stack Overflow and Reddit's r/data science.

- Webinars and Workshops: Attend webinars and workshops conducted by industry experts to stay updated on the latest trends and technologies.

Success Story of transition from Java developer to Data Scientist

Tom, a Java application developer was working in a small-scale company. He developed a keen interest in the data science area. It became his passion with high priority.

Tom enrolled in an Industrial institute giving formal training in Data Science. He learned Python and SQL to get a deep understanding. He grasped the advanced data structures and algorithms. He grasped Machine Learning in Python mastering advanced statistical techniques and predictive modelling. Tom adopted the TensorFlow framework very well. He achieved 10+ certifications in Data Science, Data platform, AI fundamentals, Machine Learning, Big Data and Advanced Analytics.

Tom took up a stretch assignment to work on a project that had Data Science implementation. It turned out to be an easy way for him for the transition. Worth noting!!

Conclusion

Transitioning from a Developer to a Data Scientist requires a strategic approach. This process involves acquiring new skills, gaining practical experience, and leveraging your existing talents and network. By following these strategies, IT professionals can successfully navigate their career transitions and thrive in the high-demand field of Data Science. With these steps in mind, developers can make a smooth transition into data science roles, opening up greater career opportunities and advancing their professional growth to new heights.

Moving into Leadership and Management Roles

With the Technical roles, the professional is working within his techno-boundaries, with his colleagues and may have some interaction with the business teams. With managerial or leadership roles, the professional must become more extroverted and align his thought process to the organizational goals. The transition from a technical role to a managerial or leadership position in IT involves a significant shift in responsibilities, skills, and mainly the mindset. We will explore the strategies and possible actions for IT professionals to prepare for it, considering career advancement.

Understanding the Transition from Technical Roles to Management

- Intersection of Skills: The Developer or Technical leader role would give exposure to the technology and system aspects, and some interaction with the business team. Communication skills, stakeholder interaction, and teamwork at a small level could be developed with the techno roles, which can be useful as groundwork for managerial and leadership roles.

- Skill Divergence: Technical roles focus on hands-on analytics and development, while management or leadership roles emphasize strategic planning, organizational goals, and interface to the management and clients, driving the delivery.

Strategies for a Successful Transition

a. Develop Leadership and Management Skills:

- Soft Skills: Enhance your communication, especially public speaking, skills should be developed.

- Project Management: Proficiency in project management methodologies (e.g., Agile, Scrum, PMP) should be achieved.

The planning, tracking, financial management, and management reporting aspects should be imbibed well.

- Business Acumen: Understand and adopt the business skills of IT, including budgeting, ROI analysis, and strategic planning and tracking. Skills with experience in risk-taking, negotiation, and stakeholder management should be developed.

b. Pursue Relevant Education and Training:

- Advanced Degrees: Consider pursuing higher education with an MBA or a master's in information technology management.

- Certifications: Achieve Industry certifications like ITIL, PMP, or Certified ScrumMaster (CSM) to demonstrate your management capabilities. For that, you may be required to attend vendor-driven training programs or self-study to a great extent.

- Workshops and Seminars: Attend in-organization or institute-driven, leadership workshops, webinars, and industry conferences to stay updated on best practices, industry trends and networking.

c. Gain Practical Management Experience:

- Take up Leadership Roles: With profound experience, volunteer for team lead or project manager positions within your current role.

- Mentorship: Seek out mentors who are experienced IT managers to provide guidance and advice.

- Cross-Functional Projects: Participate in projects that require collaboration across different departments to broaden your organizational and stakeholder understanding.

d. Build a Strong Professional Network:

- Networking: Connect with senior IT leaders and managers through LinkedIn, industry associations, and professional events.

- Professional Associations: Join organizations with membership for the Project Management Institute (PMI) or the Association for Computing Machinery (ACM) for networking opportunities and referring various resources.

e. Explore Organizational Dynamics:

- Company Culture: Familiarize yourself with your organization's culture, values, and goals. You should be familiar with the vertical or matrix organization structure, and the nitty-gritties of it.

- Stakeholder Management: Learn to identify and manage the expectations of various stakeholders, including executives, clients, and team members.

f. Exhibit Leadership Qualities:

- Proactive Initiative: Analise the current state and Identify problems along with possible remedies, showing your readiness to take on more responsibility.

- Team Development: Take Radical steps for team building, promoting a collaborative environment, and guiding junior colleagues.

- Decision-Making: Make informed decisions with calculated risks, balancing client requirements with organizational objectives.

g. Update as latest at Resume and Online Profiles:

- Resume: Emphasize leadership roles, project management experience, and any relevant certifications or degrees.

- Online Profiles: Update your LinkedIn profile to reflect your career aspirations and management skills. LinkedIn provides services for job search and leads for the right role as per your aspirations and management skills.

h. Prepare for Management Interviews:

- Leadership skills: Remain ready to project yourself with leadership skills, managerial experiences, and stakeholder and team management strategies. Some ready stories of success to be put up at the interview, that can appreciate your profile and experience.

- Situation-Based Questions: Prepare to answer questions about how you would manage specific management challenges or scenarios.

Additional Resources:

- Training / Certifications: PMI PMP, PgMP Course and Certification,

- Blogs and Forums: Follow blogs like IBM Business Value (IBV), and Harvard Business Review and participate in forums like LinkedIn groups focused on IT leadership.

- Webinars and Workshops: Actively participate in events hosted by Institutes, and industry leaders to gain insights and practical advice.

Success Story of transition from Technical to Manager position

Mahesh, a technical leader, was seeking career advancement. He was working on a mid-size web technology project that involved technical complexities. He aspired to become a Project Manager for a more complex project. Mahesh had a solid understanding of the Software Development Life Cycle (SDLC) and was actively collaborating with stakeholders for requirements gathering and product reviews.

Recognizing the skill gaps needed to transition to a Project Manager role, Mahesh conducted a self-assessment. He then studied the Project Management Body of Knowledge (PMBOK) and pursued training in project and finance management. Additionally, he focused on developing his soft skills, such as negotiation and presentation skills.

As a next step, Mahesh obtained PMI certification to validate his knowledge and skills. He also took on a shadow assignment to learn from an experienced Project Manager on a live project, which provided him with valuable insights into the PM role. Ultimately, Mahesh was able to secure a position as a Project Manager.

Conclusion

Despite the popular saying that "leaders are born," leadership skills can actually be developed through training and experience. Transitioning into leadership and management roles in IT requires a blend of technical knowledge, management skills, and strategic thinking. By embracing these strategies, IT professionals can navigate their career transitions more effectively and emerge as successful leaders in the IT industry. These approaches not only enhance their career advancement prospects but also increase their impact within their organizations.

Transitioning from Technical to Strategic Positions

The strategic positions require a different thought process, strategic approach, risk-taking mindset and negotiation and persuasion skills. The transition from technical to strategic positions would require the IT professional to develop experience in wide areas of management, technical acumen, and executive stakeholder management. We will explore this type of transition.

Prepare for Technical to Strategic Position Transition

a. Visualize the wider Picture:

- Business Acumen: You should gain a deep understanding of your organization's business model, industry trends, and competitive landscape. Learn how your technical expertise aligns with and supports the broader organizational business goals.

- Client-Centric Focus: Align your focus from purely technical solutions to understanding customer needs and how your and teams' work impacts their user experience and satisfaction. Client satisfaction is the necessary code word for ultimate success.

b. Build Leadership Skills:

- Communication: Communication skills are extremely important for Strategic leadership. Public speaking along with presentation skills, writing skills and active listening skills should be at par with any Leader. There are various executive training programs, which should be opted for by the IT professional to develop leadership skills.

- Decision-making and risk-taking: The Leaders are required to take certain high-level decisions. Usually, it is done with statistical data input, with calculated risk. These are crucial traits of an excellent leader. It requires a deep understanding of the business, the client's needs, and the market insight.

- Influence and Persuasion: It's important to influence and persuade others, that includes clients, management, colleagues, and the reporting teams. This, in essence, involves negotiating, forming alliances, and establishing the value of your proposal or ideas.

c. Building a Strategic Network:

- Cross-Sector Relationships: You would develop strong relationships across various industry departments within the organization. Understand their goals and challenges to identify areas where IT can add strategic value.

- Industry Networks: Collaborate with industry groups, attend conferences, and participate in professional networks to stay updated on market trends and best practices. This can also provide new perspectives and innovative ideas, to leverage for your clients and business.

d. Project Management and Execution

- Strategic Projects: To have a strategic impact on the organization, you should get involved in high-focus projects. This helps in understanding how strategic decisions are taken and executed.

- Critical Resource Management: The critical resources need to be managed well with sensitivity. These include budget, personnel, and time, to achieve organizational strategic objectives effectively.

e. Adhere Change Management:

- Adaptability: One should remain open to change and willing to adapt to new strategies, processes, and technologies. It should be percolated well to the clients, management and project teams, to seek the required results. The leader should lead by example and support the teams through business cycles.

- Innovation: Innovation is a need of the time, as productivity and KPI efficiency are required to be achieved to sustain the business. This includes fostering a culture where new ideas are openly supported and implemented.

Developing Strategic Thinking Skills

Strategic thinking requires a mindset change. We shall see how it can be developed.

a. Vision and Strategy:

- Vision and Planning: The Leader should have an organizational vision for the near term and long term, as to how the organization and project teams should navigate the business. One should think beyond the present and look for near-term and long-term plans. Think beyond the present and plan for the long term. Consider how current trends and technologies might evolve and impact your organization in the future.

- Strategic outlook: Adopting appropriate strategy, the leader should focus on organizational business goals and create business value. Anticipating various future business possibilities, the strategies for different potential outcomes should be formulated.

b. Critical thought process:

- Analysis: The Leader should have the ability to analyse complex problems, identify key issues, and understand the implications of different solutions. This would involve evaluating risks and benefits.

- Problem-Solving: Focus on issue resolution at a strategic level, rather than addressing a piecemeal basis short-sighted mitigation.

c. Decision-Making:

- Data-Driven Decisions: The statistical data and analytics can be utilized for making informed strategic decisions. This will involve certain calculated business risks to be taken. The business KPI's metrics should be understood well to adopt appropriate business options.

- Unbiased Judgement: The leader should have certain insight with intuition for the business situations. The judgement for a decision should utilise an analytical and intuitive thought process.

d. Practical Approach:

- Integration: The leader should integrate various areas of knowledge and expertise and come up with comprehensive strategies. This involves understanding how various functions within the organization have dependencies and collaborate.

- Systemic Thinking: One should adopt a systemic thinking approach to understand the complex mutual dependencies within the organization and its environment.

Conclusion

Techno-managerial executive roles, such as CxO positions, are highly sought after in any organization. Combining the right skills and capabilities can help individuals advance their careers. By focusing on strategic skill development and gaining relevant experience, IT professionals can successfully transition from technical roles to organizational leadership positions. This shift enables them to contribute significantly to the success of the organization.

Handling Career Plateaus and Seeking New Challenges

Many IT Professionals face stagnation in the middle part of their careers. If appropriate opportunities with the right business-oriented skill development and certain management support *(read as luck)* are not attained, then sustaining the career can have high risk. This can happen because of cost optimization exercises taking place, in the organizations. So, essentially every IT Professional should always remain on tows, and upskill or reskill in the current and upcoming business technology and leadership skills, gain relevant experience in those areas, keeping all senses open. We shall see how to explore opportunities within career plateaus or stagnation states, that can help you navigate to have a sustained career graph, in a systematic way.

Steps to address Career stagnation

a. Self-Assessment:

- Assess Current Role: Evaluate your current role and responsibilities. Identify what aspects of your Job, you are confident in and which areas you are underutilized.

- Identify Strengths and Weaknesses: Carry out the SWOT analysis for yourself. This will give you Insight into your capabilities and lacunas. And you can plan better for your skills development.

b. Set SMART Goals:

- Professional Development: Based on the swot analysis, define SMART goals (Specific, Measurable, Achievable, Relevant, and Time-bound) for your professional development. This could include studying business trends, adopting new technologies, taking up technical or management certifications, and improving on much-required soft skills.

- Career Advancement: Define your career aspirations. What you would want to achieve in the near time and long term. Accordingly, define realistic goals. Do you require organization change? If you want to continue in your current organization, what would be the avenues and approaches to be adopted? What horizontal or lateral move you could achieve? What can be motivational factors, that you should drive yourself to further your career?

c. Enhance Skills:

- Consistent Learning: Study the organizational learnings, take up new technology courses, attend Workshops, and participate in webinars relevant to your field. Educating yourself with new skills can avail new opportunities and make your role more exciting.

- Cross-training: Gain experience in different areas of your organization. This could involve working on cross-functional projects or temporarily joining another team to broaden your expertise.

d. Seek Feedback and Mentoring:

- Constructive Feedback: You should regularly seek feedback from your manager, colleagues, and mentors. Assess yourself, how you are perceived and where you can improvise.

- Mentoring: Identify a mentor who can provide guidance, share their experiences, and help you come out of your career stagnation. A mentor can provide a new outlook and advice on overcoming lacunas to move ahead.

e. Take up New Challenges:

- New Opportunities: Come out of your comfort zone and take up new opportunities for new projects or initiatives within your organization. This can give you opportunities and challenges, to demonstrate and develop your capabilities.

- Leadership assignments: Go for leadership roles, even if they may be formal or informal. Leading a team or a project can help you develop new skills and attain depth and recognition.

f. Collaborate to win:

- Organizational Networking: Develop cross-departmental relationships with colleagues. Becoming aware of various organizational domains can provide new insights and opportunities.

- Exterior Networking: You can increase awareness and skills by attending industry conferences, joining professional institute memberships, and actively participating in online forums. The networking can lead to new avenues and keep you well-informed about industry trends.

Identifying and Overcoming Career Stagnation

Career stagnation is a common experience in which an employee feels that he is stuck up for professional growth, progress or advancement within the organization. The professional feels a lack of new challenges or opportunities. This can lead to a lack of motivation and a decrease in job satisfaction, which can have a significant business impact on productivity and organizational success.

Addressing career stagnation has become an important part of organizational development. The manager of a professional may want to ensure that the employee is engaged well with the business and that he is learning and growing as the business evolves.

The professional must make out the stagnation and take active steps to come out of it. You will be required to collaborate more, find out some leads within the business lines, get the opportunities and take it forward to succeed in the further path. We would explore the ways and steps to achieve it.

a. Read the Signs of Stagnation:

- Lack of Motivation: Feeling unmotivated or disinterested in your work can be a sign of stagnation.

- No Career Progression: If you haven't had any promotions or new responsibilities for a significant period, you might be experiencing stagnation.

- Skill Plateau: When you're not learning new skills or your current skills are not being utilized, it's a sign that you need new challenges.

b. Conduct Root Cause Analysis:

- Organizational Hurdles: Sometimes stagnation is due to organizational issues such as limited opportunities for advancement or a lack of support for professional development. These are Inherent obstacles and one should make a timely decision to change the department or organization.

- Personal Constraints: Personal factors such as fear of change, lack of confidence, or comfort zone lockup situation can also contribute to career stagnation.

c. Plan to eradicate stagnation:

- Set practical goals: Define what you want to achieve in your career and set clear, actionable goals to further your career.

- Seek Opportunities for Progress: Explore the opportunities within your organization or consider Opportunities in the outside world. This might include new companies, roles, projects, or even domains or industries.

- Increase Your Visibility: Increase your visibility within your organization by publishing your achievements, taking stretch assignments for high-visibility projects, and building a self-brand with a go-to expert in your area.

d. Take the help of Professional Development Resources:

- Training Programs: You could take up organizational training programs. Or else you can explore outside market external courses and certifications, based on budgetary considerations.

- Professional Institutes: You can take membership in professional associations related to your domain. These institutes provide resources such as training, certification programs, and networking opportunities.

e. Consider Career Coaching:

- Career Coaches: A career coach can help you identify your career goals, guide you to develop a plan to achieve them and provide support and accountability along the way.

- Peer Groups: Join peer groups or mastermind groups where you can share experiences, challenges, and solutions with others in similar situations.

> There is a bit of difference in Coaching v/s mentoring… While the Mentor would belong to your domain/skills area and can handhold your skill development, the Coach can be an external person, who would have a higher perspective and will guide you to define and achieve your goals, to achieve the required progress promptly.

f. Review and Adapt the change:

- Regular Review: You can regularly take time to review your career progress and update your goals and strategies as required. The unbiased critical self-assessment helps achieve larger goals.

- Adapt the change: Always remain open to upcoming change and willing to adapt to it, based on new skills and experiences.

Success Story of Overcoming Career Stagnation

Alan, a project manager with over five years of experience, found himself stagnating in his career due to an industry recession. While his project delivery work was satisfactory and he effectively managed his assigned state, it lacked the challenges necessary for career advancement. His manager was preoccupied with various job complexities, leaving Alan without the guidance he needed to explore growth opportunities. Sensing that he was stuck in his career, Alan felt low and demotivated, prompting him to take action.

He conducted a self-assessment and identified gaps in his skills. Subsequently, he engaged with a career coach who advised him to focus on upskilling and preparing for advanced project and program management roles. Alan enrolled in a soft skills training program at an industrial institute to adopt a growth mindset. He also received training to enhance his public speaking, presentation skills, and strategic interview techniques, which boosted his confidence and improved his motivation.

In pursuit of further growth, Alan earned a program management certification, completing it with flying colours. He reactivated his LinkedIn profile and began sharing even his small achievements. The appreciation he received from peers and friends helped rebuild his confidence. Additionally, Alan paid more attention to his health by incorporating regular exercise into his routine.

After upgrading his skills, Alan created a GitHub profile showcasing his experience, achievements, and certifications. Once he published his CV, opportunities in program management began to arise. Eventually, he secured a challenging assignment in program management, marking the next step in his career. Kudos to Alan!

Conclusion

If you can recognize career stagnation early and proactively plan for skill and role upgrades based on available opportunities, you can overcome it and continue to excel both professionally and personally. It's important to view challenges or adverse conditions as opportunities and turn them into successes. This approach will lead to job satisfaction and open up further career growth opportunities.

Chapter 9

Align with Industry Trends

As the IT industry evolves rapidly, it is essential to stay current with the latest developments in technology and management. IT professionals need to put in extra effort to adapt to these changes and navigate the inherent competition from peers and new entrants. There are various ways to master these trends, which we will explore here.

Staying up to date with Industry Trends

With the rapid changes in the industry, it becomes an ongoing challenge to adapt to the latest technologies and stay relevant in the industry. Here are some of the ways to achieve it.

a. Continuing Professional Development (CPD):

   - Institutional Online Training and Certifications: The established IT Institutes conduct various training and certification programs. These have tied up with brand organizations such as IBM, Microsoft, and Amazon among others. You should register for career-relevant courses on platforms like Coursera, Pluralsight, or Udacity. Most of these platforms offer certifications that can enhance your skills, knowledge, and credentials. And your skills are validated with the certification.

- Seminars and Workshops: The IT Theme-based seminars and workshops are becoming norms of the industry. It gives opportunities to enhance your knowledge, and at the same time, collaborate with industry experts and peers. You can get good exposure to the latest trends in technologies and methodologies. The workshop can provide an opportunity for good understanding and experience.

b. Industry Conferences and Meetups:

- IT Industry Conferences: The industry conferences often feature presenters and sponsors, highlighting new products and services. This provides the opportunity to get exposure to the latest technologies and innovations in the field. It is a subtle way to stay up to date on new tools and solutions that can improve your work and experiences. You can participate in industry conferences such as AWS re: Invent, Google Cloud Next, or Microsoft Ignite. Such events provide insights into the current trends and future directions in the industry.

- Meetups: The Meetup is a social platform for hosting and organizing in-person and virtual activities, gatherings, and events for people and communities of similar interests, and professions. You can join local meetups or online groups focused on your area of expertise and aspiration. Meetup.com and similar platforms can provide you with avenues to find groups and events that match your pursuits.

c. Webinars and Podcasts:

- Webinars: The webinars are typically live events, and often incorporate interactive elements like live chat, Q&A sessions, polls, surveys etc. You should regularly attend webinars hosted by technology companies, educational institutions, and industry organizations. These often cover new products, technologies, and best practices. This can help enhance your knowledge and awareness of the various products and trends.

- Podcasts: The podcasts are pre-recorded and available for download or streaming at any time. You should listen to industry-specific podcasts during your commute or workout. Podcasts such as "The Cloudcast," "Software Engineering Daily," and "The Changelog" offer valuable insights and interviews with IT industry leaders and subject matter experts.

d. Book Reading and Research Papers:

- Books: The books provide plenty of knowledge on umpteen areas. You could develop a regular reading habit, which can give you immense know-how in various skill areas. You can read books by industry experts and thought leaders. Some essential reads include "The Phoenix Project" by Gene Kim, Kevin Behr, and George Spafford, and "Clean Code" by Robert C. Martin.

- Research Articles: The research is carried out to validate current technology, and methodology and create or propose current trends to it. It would provide insight into the latest upcoming technologies. You should review scholarly articles and research papers from sources like IBV, IEEE, and ACM to stay well aware of innovative technology and developments in it.

Developing the skill of rapid reading can be an enjoyable hobby. It involves adopting specific techniques that anyone can learn. Rapid reading is an effective way to enhance your reading speed and comprehension. When practised regularly, this hobby can become a beneficial habit that positively impacts your overall career. In his book "Atomic Habits", James Clear discusses how small changes can lead to significant results over time. You could refer to enjoy it.

Keeping Up with Technological Advancements

It is very much essential that you keep up pace with the technology advancements. We will explore the ways to do it.

a. Practical knowledge:

- Sandbox Environments: Use online sandbox environments to experiment with new technologies. The various cloud platforms like AWS, Azure, and Google Cloud offer free tiers and credits for learning purposes.

- Stretch Projects: You can work on personal or open-source projects to apply newly attained skills and technologies in real-world developments.

b. Latest Certifications:

- Platform Certifications: You can obtain certifications from major tech companies like AWS, Google, Microsoft, and Cisco and PMI in a PM career. These certifications often cover the latest advancements and best practices in their respective technologies and management streams.

- Niche skills Certifications: Consider certifications in the latest hot skills such as cybersecurity, AI, and data science. Organizations like CompTIA, ISC2, and the Data Science Council of America avail relevant certifications.

c. Communities and Forums:

- Stack Overflow and GitHub: You can participate in discussions on online platforms like Stack Overflow and GitHub. These communities have a mission to help empower the world to develop technology through collective knowledge. These communities have huge documentation on various technologies with practical experience and case studies. It can provide insight to your queries and highlight real-world applications of modern technologies.

- Reddit and Quora: You can follow subreddits and topics related to your field on Reddit and Quora. These platforms have active discussions on the latest trends and technologies.

Following Industry News and Updates

The industry news updates are another way of keeping up with the industry trends. It can provide insight into the latest trends and ways to align yourself with the industry and organizations.

a. News Websites and Blogs:

- Technical News: You can regularly visit websites like TechCrunch, Wired, ZDNet, and Ars Technica for the latest news and analysis on technology trends.

- Industry Blogs: You can follow blogs from industrial leaders, SMEs and organizations in your industry. You can refer to the Google Cloud Blog, Microsoft Azure Blog, and AWS News Blog among others.

b. Newsletters and Mailing Lists:

- Newsletters: You can subscribe to email newsletters from reputable sources such as The Information, Hacker News Digest, and O'Reilly Media. These newsletters contain the most important news and trends.

- Platform Updates: You can sign up for newsletters from technology vendors and industry organizations to receive updates on new products, services, and events.

c. Social Media and Professional Platforms:

- Twitter and LinkedIn: You should follow industry leaders, companies, and groups on Twitter and LinkedIn. You can engage with their posts and participate in discussions to stay informed and connected.

- YouTube Channels: You can subscribe to YouTube channels that focus on technology news and tutorials. Channels like Linus Tech Tips, The Verge, and Tech with Tim provide insightful content.

d. Trend Reports and Whitepapers:

- Business Reports: You should refer to the business review reports from industry analysts like Gartner, Forrester, and IDC. These reports provide an in-depth analysis of overall industry trends and forecasts.

- Whitepapers: You can read whitepapers from technology companies and research institutions. These documents often detail recent technologies, statistical analysis with use cases, and implementation approaches.

By exploring these resources and strategies, IT professionals can stay current with industry trends, keep up with technological advancements, and follow industry news and updates to understand the intricacies of the industry.

Role of Professional Associations and Conferences

The Associations and Conferences provide avenues for gaining industry insight, trends and networking opportunities with industry leaders, peers, and subject matter experts.

Professional Associations

There are a lot of advantages to joining professional associations. It helps in developing your career. We shall refer to it here.

a. Networking Opportunities:

- Collaborations: The professional associations provide a platform for IT professionals to connect with peers, industry leaders, and potential mentors. These connections can lead to new opportunities, collaborations, and acquaintances.

- Discussion Forums: The professional associations have online forums, special study groups, and local chapters, where members can exchange views on trends, challenges, and solutions.

b. Access to Resources:

- Educational Materials: The associations offer a wealth of resources including research papers, industry reports, whitepapers, and case studies that can help members stay informed about the current trends and developments in the industry and domains within it.

- Training Programs: The associations provide training programs, webinars, workshops, and certification courses to help members enhance their skills and knowledge.

c. Professional Development:

- Certifications and Credentials: The certifications from professional associations can enhance your credibility and demonstrate your expertise to employers and clients.

- Career Services: The career-oriented service associations offer career services such as job boards, resume reviews, and career counselling, to support members in their career advancement.

d. Expertise and Representation:

- Industry Standards: The professional associations are often involved in defining industry standards and best practices, providing expertise to ensure the members adhere to high professional and ethical standards.

- Policy Influence: These organizations often advise on behalf of their members, influencing public policy and regulations that affect the overall industry.

Conferences

The conferences are a way to collaborate and get exposure to the latest trends in the industry. We will see the benefits of attending conferences.

a. Collaborate and Learn:

  • Workshops and Sessions: The conferences offer a variety of sessions, including workshops, keynote speeches, and breakout sessions, where attendees can get to know about the latest technologies, methodologies, and industry trends.

  • Hands-On Labs: Some conferences include hands-on labs where attendees can get practical experience with new tools and technologies. These are very useful, especially for the new technology areas.

b. Networking:

  • Meet and Greet: The conferences provide opportunities to meet leaders, peers, and subject matter experts in person, which can lead to valuable business connections, partnerships, and alliances.

  • Exhibitions and Vendor Booths: The attendees can interact with vendors and service providers, discovering new products, services, and solutions that can benefit their work.

c. Industry Insights and Trends:

  • Keynote Speeches: Industry leaders often present keynote speeches that provide insights into the future of the industry, emerging trends, and strategic direction.

  • Panel Discussions: Panels featuring experts and thought leaders can provide diverse perspectives on critical issues facing the industry.

d. Professional Recognition:

  • Awards and Recognition: The conferences can include award ceremonies that recognize outstanding contributions and achievements in the industry, providing a platform for professionals to gain recognition and visibility across the industry platforms.

Benefits of Joining IT Associations

Joining IT Associations has varied benefits and can help in multiple ways to build skills and achieve career advancement opportunities.

a. Career Advancement:

- Networking: A strong professional network built through association membership, can lead to job opportunities, mentorship, and collaborations.

- Professional Recognition: Membership and active participation can enhance your professional exposure, reputation, and visibility within the industry.

b. Skill Enhancement:

- Training and Certifications: Access to various special training and certification programs can be availed. It can help you stay current with the latest skills and technologies, making you more competitive in the job market.

- Continuing Education: The associations offer continuous learning opportunities, ensuring you can keep up with industry advancements.

c. Access to Information:

- Industry News: You can stay informed about the latest industry news, trends, and research through association publications, newsletters, and online resources.

- Best Practices: You can learn about industry best practices and standards that can improve your work and you can contribute to the performance improvement of your projects and organization.

d. Community and Support:

- Peer Support: As part of the professional community, you can get a support network, where you can seek advice, share experiences, and find encouragement.

- Mentorship Opportunities: Some associations offer formal and informal mentorship programs where you can gain guidance from more experienced professionals.

e. Discounts and Perks:

- Event Discounts: The members often receive discounts on conference registration fees, training programs, and other association-sponsored events.

- Publications and Resources: You can gain free or discounted access to industry publications, research reports, and other valuable resources.

Examples of Prominent IT Associations

- PMI – Project Management Institute: The well-known institute in Project management. It offers various PM training and certifications like PMP, ACP, and DASSM. The PMBOK from PMI has assumed high significance and serves as an industry benchmark.

- ACM (Association for Computing Machinery): It focuses on advancing computing as a science and profession.

- IEEE Computer Society: It offers resources and networking for professionals in computer science and engineering.

- ISACA: It specializes in IT governance, risk management, and cybersecurity.

- CompTIA: It is known for its certifications and resources for IT professionals.

- (ISC)^2: If focuses on cybersecurity, offering certifications like the CISSP.

Conclusion

IT professionals can benefit from professional associations and conferences. By participating, they can significantly enhance their exposure to technology trends, career opportunities, and build a supportive network of peers and mentors.

Leveraging Industry Publications and Online Resources

For IT professionals, staying informed and continuously learning is necessary. Leveraging industry publications and online resources helps in keeping up with the latest trends, technologies, and best practices. Here is how to effectively utilize these resources:

Benefits of Using Industry Publications and Online Resources

There would be numerous benefits to using industry publications and online resources.

You should take advantage of it and improve your skills and career opportunities.

a. Staying Current:

- It helps to remain up to date with the latest innovations in technology and industry trends.

- Understand emerging technologies and how they might impact your domain areas.

b. Professional Development:

- Get insights into best practices and methodologies.

- Upgrade knowledge and skills through articles, published papers, and industrial domain information.

c. Networking and Community:

- Engage with peers, and colleagues through community, forums, and social media discussions.

- Actively participate in discussions and share your knowledge and experiences.

d. Research and Problem Solving:

- Evolve solutions to technical problems through case studies, whitepapers, and research articles.

- Exchange views and learn from the experiences of peers; apply the lesson learned to your projects.

Recommended Blogs, Journals, and Websites

There are numerous sources for blogs, journals, and various websites. We will refer to some of these as ready examples to explore and follow.

Blogs

a. TechCrunch:

- It covers the latest technology news, startups, and product launches.

- It gives the advantage of staying updated with industry trends and new technologies.

b. Ars Technica:

- It focuses on technology, science, and IT policy news.

- It provides detailed analysis and reviews of new technologies.

c. Hackaday:

- It covers a wide range of topics including hardware, software, and DIY projects.

- It's Ideal for professionals looking to explore and experiment with innovative ideas.

d. Krebs on Security:

- This is a blog by Brian Krebs, focusing on cybersecurity news and analysis.

- It is essential for IT professionals concerned with security and data protection.

Journals

There are established institutes, which publish industrial journals, which provide high information and knowledge about various IT industry-related topics.

a. IEEE Computer Society Digital Library:

  - It provides access to a treasure of research papers, articles, and information regarding conferences, in computer science and engineering.

  - It helps with deep technical research and remaining well aware-of academic advancements.

b. ACM Digital Library:

  - It has a vast collection of articles, papers, and conference information from the Association for Computing Machinery.

  - It is ideal for researching and understanding the theoretical details of the latest technologies.

c. Journal of Information Technology:

  - It offers insights into IT management, systems, and technologies.

  - It is useful for evaluating the impact of IT on business and management practices.

Websites

a. Stack Overflow:

  - This is a community-driven Q&A site for programmers and IT professionals.

  - It is excellent for finding solutions to coding problems and learning from the community.

b. GitHub:

- This is a platform for version control and collaboration, hosting millions of open-source projects.

- It is very useful for exploring code, contributing to projects, and learning through collaboration.

c. Reddit (Subreddits like r/technology, r/programming, r/sysadmin):

- These are community-driven forums where professionals discuss technology, programming, and system administration.

- It provides a mix of news, discussions, and advice from experts.

d. Hacker News:

- This is a social news website focusing on computer science and entrepreneurship.

- It offers a variety of news articles, discussions, and personal stories from the tech community.

e. InfoQ:

- This is a resource for software development news, articles, and events.

- It covers topics like software architecture, cloud computing, AI, and DevOps.

Conclusion

IT professionals can stay updated on the latest trends and developments in their field by utilizing resources such as industry publications, blogs, journals, and websites. This ongoing learning can greatly enhance their career advancement and skill development.

Chapter 10

Future Trends and Forecast

The technology and management sectors within the IT industry are evolving rapidly. Emerging technologies are transforming the entire industry, making it essential for professionals to understand future trends and their impact on IT careers to remain relevant and competitive.

Digital transformation and artificial intelligence (AI) have become vital for companies seeking to maintain competitiveness and drive growth. Embracing digital transformation is no longer optional; it is a necessity for organizations aiming to adapt to changing customer expectations, optimize operations, and leverage emerging technologies. In this context, we will explore new technologies and their effects on professionals in the field.

Impact of Emerging Technologies on IT Careers

a. Artificial Intelligence and Machine Learning:

- Generative AI: Tools like ChatGPT and IBM watsonx are revolutionizing the way we interact with machines. Generative AI can create content, automate tasks, and provide sophisticated insights, which means professionals need to be proficient in AI/ML algorithms and applications. The business opportunity with Gen AI is expected to grow to a very high extent.

- **Career Impact:** The increased demand for AI specialists, data scientists, and machine learning engineers is expected. The Professionals in all IT roles will need to understand how to leverage AI to improve processes and decision-making. The entire industry is adopting the Gen AI in a highly positive way. That will drive the next upcoming technology transformation cycle. It will change how the business is run by the clients across the world. And obviously, it will drive the way of working for IT professionals as well.

b. Quantum Computing:

- **Breakthroughs in Computing Power:** Quantum computing has a tremendous ability to solve overly complex problems much faster than classical computers. This technology will impact fields in various areas and many ways - like cryptography, materials science, and optimization problems.

- **Career Impact:** There will be new opportunities for quantum programmers, researchers, and engineers. The IT professionals will need to understand quantum principles and how these can be implemented in various industries. Very few industry players are in this domain, and it is expected to increase dramatically in the coming time.

c. Blockchain and Decentralized Technologies:

- **Beyond Cryptocurrencies:** Blockchain technology is already in high use for more than just cryptocurrencies. Its applications in supply chain management, healthcare, and finance are growing.

- **Career Impact:** The demand for blockchain developers, security experts, and blockchain project managers will increase. The professionals will need to understand decentralized networks, smart contracts, and cryptographic principles.

d. Internet of Things (IoT):

-   Connected Devices: The IoT connects everyday objects to the internet, allowing for real-time data collection and automation. This technology is getting integrated into smart homes, cities, and industries.

-   Career Impact: There will be an increased need for IoT architects, data analysts, and cybersecurity experts. While taking advantage of the opportunities, understanding the IoT protocols, data management, and security will be very essential.

e. Edge Computing:

-   Processing Power on the Edge: Edge computing involves processing data closer to where it gets generated, reducing latency and bandwidth use. This is essential for applications like autonomous vehicles and real-time analytics.

-   Career Impact: The opportunities for edge computing specialists, network engineers, and systems architects are expected to increase. It can remain as a niche area of skills. The professionals will be required to be proficient in edge computing frameworks and real-time data processing.

f. 5G and Beyond:

-   Enhanced Connectivity: The 5G technology promises faster speeds, higher data bandwidth, lower latency, and the ability to connect more devices. This will enable new applications in VR/AR, smart cities, and remote healthcare.

-   Career Impact: The demand for network engineers, telecom experts, and application developers who can leverage 5G capabilities is bound to increase. An understanding of 5G infrastructure and its applications will be necessary though. Higher than 5G technology can come up in the future, and IT professionals are required to be ready for any upcoming change.

g. Cybersecurity:

  - Wide range of Threats: As technology evolves, so do the vulnerabilities and threats. Cybersecurity will continue to be a top priority with the rise of sophisticated attacks and the expansion of the attack surface.

  - Career Impact: There is already a growing need for cybersecurity analysts, ethical hackers, and security architects. Continuous learning about new vulnerabilities, threats and security measures will be necessary, as well as solutions for them in a highly demanding timeline.

h. Sustainable Technologies

  - Green IT: There is a growing emphasis on sustainability in technology. The Green IT practices aim to reduce the environmental impact of computing.

  - Career Impact: The roles of sustainability officers, green IT specialists, and energy-efficient systems designers are expected to rise. The professionals will be required to understand sustainable practices and technologies, and the implementation approaches. These are evolving technologies so that more rapid changes in innovation and technology can take place in the coming time.

Exploring Specific Technologies

We will explore the upcoming technologies for the capability and skills needed to cope with the change.

a. Generative AI (ChatGPT, IBM watsonx):

  - Capabilities: These AI models can generate human-like text, assist in customer service, automate content creation, and provide insights from data.

  - Skills Needed: Proficiency will be required in natural language processing (NLP), AI ethics, and the integration of AI tools into business processes.

b. Quantum Computing:

- Capabilities: The quantum computers can perform very complex calculations at unprecedented speeds, impacting cryptography, complex simulations, and optimization problems.

- Skills Needed: The understanding of quantum algorithms, quantum programming languages like Qiskit, and familiarity with quantum hardware will be required to be required. These are still upcoming technologies, so more innovation is expected in the time to come.

c. Blockchain:

- Capabilities: The Blockchain is a shared, immutable ledger that facilitates the process of recording transactions and tracking assets in a business network. The Blockchain ensures secure, transparent, and tamper-proof transactions and data management.

- Skills Needed: The knowledge of blockchain frameworks (e.g., Ethereum, Hyperledger), smart contract development, and decentralized application (dApp) creation will be required to adapt well. The technology is expected to evolve soon.

d. Internet of Things (IoT):

- Capabilities: The IoT enables the connection and communication of devices, facilitating automation and data collection for smarter decision-making.

- Skills Needed: Proficiency in IoT platforms, sensor integration, and data analytics will be required to be developed. These will remain niche skills and are expected to grow in the near time.

e. Edge Computing:

- Capabilities: Edge computing processes data locally on devices, reducing latency and bandwidth requirements.

- Skills Needed: Expertise in edge computing architectures, real-time data processing, and network optimization will be required to be developed.

f. 5G Technology:

- Capabilities: The 5G offers high-speed, higher data bandwidth, and low-latency connectivity that supports advanced applications like autonomous driving, remote surgery, and augmented reality.

- Skills Needed: The knowledge of 5G infrastructure, network management, and application development for high-bandwidth, low-latency environments will be required to assume these work areas.

Getting Ready for the Future of Work in IT

The IT professionals must be proactive in preparing for the future, as the IT industry continues to evolve. This includes adapting to new work environments, embracing technological advancements, and developing skills that will be in high demand. Here is a comprehensive guide on how IT professionals can prepare for the future of work and adapt to new work environments.

Key Trends Shaping the Future of Work in IT

a. Remote and Hybrid Work Models:

- The COVID-19 pandemic accelerated the adoption of remote and hybrid work models. These models are likely to persist, requiring IT professionals to be proficient in remote collaboration tools and practices. Some organizations are coming up with full-time roles with remote work, while some organizations are insisting the employees should come to the office. We are going through a rehaul of the way of working and it would enhance in the time to come.

b. Automation and AI Integration:

- Automation and AI are transforming many aspects of IT, from network management to software development. The in-depth understanding and leveraging of these technologies will be crucial for the professionals to take up the challenging opportunities.

c. Cybersecurity as Prime:

- With the rise of remote work and the increasing number of vulnerabilities and threats, cybersecurity has become a top priority. The IT professionals must stay updated on the latest security practices and technologies.

d. Agile and DevOps Practices:

- The Agile and DevOps methodologies are becoming industry standard in software development and IT operations, emphasizing collaboration, continuous integration, and delivery.

e. Lifelong Learning and Skill Development:

- The rapid pace of technological change means that continuous learning is essential. The IT professionals must be committed to lifelong learning to stay relevant.

Adapting to New Work Environments

Considering the future trends of technology and client expectations, the work environment is changing. The IT Professional will have to adapt to the new environments and remain productive in any work situation. We shall explore the upcoming work environmental changes and how to cope with them.

Remote and Hybrid Work

a. Set Up a Productive Workspace:

- Ergonomic Setup: Ensure your workspace is user-friendly and ergonomic to provide an efficient way of working.

- Technology: You should equip yourself with the necessary tools, such as a high-speed internet connection, a reliable computer, and collaboration software (e.g., Slack, Zoom, Microsoft Teams).

b. Master Remote Collaboration Tools:

- Adopt the remote work tools and best practices for virtual communication, project management, and file sharing.

c. Time Management and Self-Discipline:

- You should develop strong time management skills, to remain productive and maintain a healthy work-life balance. Techniques like the Pomodoro Technique or time blocking can be helpful. Taking a quick break in the continuous exhaustive work duration is always advisable.

d. Effective Communication:

- You should practice clear and concise communication. Regular check-ins with your team and using appropriate communication channels can improve collaboration. You can take up soft skills training from reputed communication training institutions, and enhance your public speaking and presentation skills, which are vital in career growth.

Embracing Technological Advancements

a. Stay Updated on Emerging Technologies:

- You should follow industry news, attend webinars, and participate in online courses to stay informed about emerging technologies like Gen AI, watsonx, blockchain, and quantum computing.

b. Develop Technical Skills:

- You should continuously update your technical skills through certifications, online courses, and hands-on projects. Platforms like Coursera, Udacity, and Pluralsight provide invaluable resources.

c. Learn Automation and AI:

- You should understand how automation and AI can improve efficiency and productivity in your field. It would help great way by learning languages like Python and tools like TensorFlow.

Enhancing Cybersecurity Awareness

a. Remain on top of Vulnerabilities and Threats:

- You should regularly update your skills and knowledge about the latest cybersecurity vulnerabilities, threats and best practices by following trusted sources like Krebs on Security or Cybersecurity & Infrastructure Security Agency (CISA).

b. Implement Security Best Practices:

- You should apply best practices such as using strong, unique passwords, enabling multi-factor authentication, and regularly updating software and systems.

c. Obtain Cybersecurity Certifications:

- You should take up certifications like Certified Information Systems Security Professional (CISSP) or Certified Ethical Hacker (CEH) to enhance your knowledge and credentials.

Embracing Agile and DevOps Practices

a. Understand Agile Methodologies:

- Learn about agile frameworks like Scrum and Kanban. Books like "Scrum: The Art of Doing Twice the Work in Half the Time" by Jeff Sutherland can be insightful. The PMI Institute offers various Agile trainings and certifications like ACP, and DASSM, which can help you establish yourself in the industry.

b. Adopt DevOps Practices:

- You should adopt DevOps tools and practices that promote continuous integration and continuous delivery (CI/CD). Tools like Jenkins, Docker, and Kubernetes are essential to be well-versed with.

c. Collaboration and Continuous Improvement:

- You should embrace a culture of collaboration with agile ceremonies, feedback with showcase, and continuous improvement. Regular retrospectives and performance reviews can help identify areas for growth.

Committing to Continuous Learning

The skills must be maintained as the latest with continuous learning. A personal commitment is required to achieve this.

a. Create a Learning Plan:

- You should develop a personal learning plan that includes short-term and long-term goals. You can identify resources and timelines for achieving these goals and track them diligently for completion.

b. Engage with Professional Communities:

- You can join professional associations, online forums, and local meetups to network with peers, share knowledge, and stay motivated.

c. Seek Mentorship and Coaching:

- You can seek mentors and coaches who can provide guidance, support, and feedback on your career development.

Strategies for Future Success

a. Adaptability and Flexibility:

- You should stay open to change and remain willing to adapt to new technologies, tools, techniques, and work practices.

b. Enhance Soft Skills:

- You should develop soft skills such as communication, leadership, and problem-solving, which are increasingly valuable in collaborative and remote work environments. Getting formal training and orientation always helps with this.

c. Personal Well-being:

- You should maintain a healthy work-life balance by setting boundaries, taking breaks, and engaging in activities outside of work that bring you joy and relaxation. Regular exercise in any form like jogging, cycling, swimming, or trekking helps. Any hobby with say reading, music or travel can as well help rejuvenate yourself in a strenuous job environment.

In brief, IT professionals can successfully navigate the future of work by embracing these strategies focusing on continuous development and thriving in evolving work environments.

Role of Ethics and Sustainability in IT Careers

As technology becomes increasingly integral to our daily lives and social functioning, the role of ethics and sustainability in IT careers is more critical than ever. IT professionals must consider the ethical implications of their work and strive to create sustainable solutions that benefit society. We will understand it more in detail.

Understanding Ethical Implications of Technology

a. Data Security and Privacy:

- Importance: Protecting user data and maintaining privacy is paramount in today's world where data breaches and cyberattacks are occurring at high frequency.

- Ethical Considerations: IT professionals must ensure to implement robust security measures, respect user privacy, and comply with regulations like GDPR and CCPA.

- Best Practices: The use of encryption, conducting regular security checks and audits, and following the Principle of Least Privilege (PoLP) to minimize access to sensitive data, can be adapted well.

b. Artificial Intelligence:

-   Importance: AI and ML are transforming industries by automating tasks and providing insights. However, that is raising ethical concerns as well.

-   Ethical Considerations: Care should be taken to ensure fairness, transparency, and accountability in AI systems. The biases should be avoided, in training data and algorithms that can lead to unfair processing of any kind.

-   Best Practices: It would be advisable to implement AI ethics guidelines, regularly test for bias, and maintain transparency about how AI decisions are made.

c. Accessibility:

-   Importance: The technology should be accessible to everyone, including those with disabilities and those in underprivileged communities. The Accessibility checks should be done with appropriate technology implementation.

-   Ethical Considerations: The Design of inclusive technologies that cater to diverse user needs and bridge the digital divide can be adopted.

-   Best Practices: It is imperative to follow accessibility standards (e.g., WCAG), consider the needs of various user groups during development, and provide affordable access to technology.

d. Intellectual Property:

-   Importance: Respect for intellectual property rights is crucial in this world driven by innovation.

-   Ethical Considerations: Take care to avoid plagiarism, respect software licenses, and give proper credit to original creators.

-   Best Practices: It is advisable to use open-source software responsibly, comply with licensing agreements, and attribute work appropriately.

e. Ethical Use of Data:

- Importance: The massive amounts of data generated and collected can be used for various purposes, but it should be ensured to have ethical use of it.

- Ethical Considerations: It is essential to avoid misuse of data, ensure data accuracy, and be transparent about data collection and usage practices.

- Best Practices: It is advisable to implement data governance frameworks, obtain informed consent from users, and regularly review data usage policies.

Sustainability in IT

Sustainability is an important aspect of IT business. With the Green Revolution going across the world, it becomes essential to adopt measures for it. Sustainable IT covers the production, use, management and disposal of information technology in a way that minimizes its impact on the environment. Let us refer to the sustainable practices and the best practices to adopt.

a. Green IT Practices:

- Importance: The environmental impact of IT operations is required to be reduced as a vital factor for sustainability.

- Sustainable Practices: One can optimize energy use, recycle electronic waste, and design energy-efficient systems.

- Best Practices: You should use energy-efficient hardware, implement virtualization to reduce physical server needs, and promote e-waste recycling programs.

b. Sustainable Software Development:

- Importance: Resource consumption can be reduced by developing the software with sustainability as a continuous reference.

- Sustainable Practices: One could write efficient code, minimize resource usage, and design for scalability.

- Best Practices: You should optimize algorithms for performance, reduce unnecessary features that load the software, and ensure compatibility with legacy hardware.

c. Cloud Computing:

- Importance: The cloud computing environment offers more efficient resource use as compared to traditional on-premises data resources.

- Sustainable Practices: One could use cloud services that focus on sustainability and energy efficiency.

- Best Practices: You should opt for cloud providers with strong environmental policies, utilize serverless architectures to reduce idle resource consumption, and leverage dynamic demand with auto-scaling.

d. Remote Work:

- Importance: To lower carbon footprints and promote a better work-life balance, commuting and travel can be reduced.

- Sustainable Practices: The organizations can implement remote work policies and use virtual collaboration tools.

- Best Practices: The organizations should encourage remote work as much as possible, utilize video conferencing to reduce commute or travel, and support a virtual workplace culture.

Strategies for IT Professionals

To maintain sustainability, IT Professionals can adopt certain strategic steps, at organizational and personal levels. Below are some examples.

a. Education in Ethics and Sustainability:

- Always refer to the latest developments in ethics and sustainability through training, certifications, and industry publications.

- Collaborate with discussions and training, on ethical situational issues and sustainability challenges in the IT industry.

b. Ethical Decision-Making Frameworks:

- Established frameworks can be used to evaluate the ethical implications of decisions at the project and organization level.

- Some examples can be the IEEE Code of Ethics and ACM Code of Ethics.

c. Responsibility as Culture:

- The organizational culture could be created and maintained for ethical behaviour and sustainability.

- The leaders can lead by example and encourage colleagues to consider the broader impact of their work.

d. Collaborate with Stakeholders:

- Ensure that ethical and sustainable practices are integrated into business processes, by working with peer groups, such as legal and compliance matters.

- Understand the perspectives and concerns of external stakeholders, including customers and community groups, by collaborating with them.

e. Innovation for Sustainability:

- A positive environmental impact should be created with the opportunities to develop or implement technologies.

- Considering the long-term effects of technology on society, innovation with sustainability should be adopted.

In Brief, IT professionals can contribute to a more responsible and sustainable technological future, by understanding and integrating ethics and sustainability into their day-to-day work.

Predictions for the Next Decade in IT

Rapid change and innovation are prominent themes in the IT industry. As we look ahead to the next decade, several key trends and technologies are expected to shape the future of IT. Understanding these trends can help professionals anticipate future career opportunities and better prepare for successful careers. We will explore these trends and their impact on IT professionals.

a. Artificial Intelligence to Become Day-to-Day Life:

- Trend: AI and ML technologies will evolve exponentially, to become more integrated into everyday business processes and applications.

- Impact: There will be an increased demand for AI specialists, data scientists, and machine learning engineers. The skills in developing, implementing, and managing AI solutions will be very critical.

b. High Growth in Quantum Computing:

- Trend: Quantum computing is expected to move from theoretical research to practical applications. This will solve problems that are currently taking longer processing time and are intractable for legacy computers.

- Impact: New career paths will emerge for quantum developers, analysts, researchers, and engineers. The IT Professionals will need to understand quantum algorithms and how to implement them in real-world scenarios.

c. Proliferation of Edge Computing and IoT:

- Trend: IoT devices will drive the need for edge computing to process data closer to its source, reducing latency and bandwidth usage.

- Impact: The skills requirements in IoT architecture, edge computing, and real-time data analytics will grow. The IT Professionals will require skills in IoT platforms, sensor integration, and edge computing frameworks.

d. Widespread Adoption of 5G and higher Technology:

- Trend: The 5G and higher technology will enable faster, more reliable internet connections, supporting new applications in autonomous vehicles, smart cities, and augmented reality.

- Impact: The opportunities and requirements will increase for network engineers, telecom experts, and application developers specializing in high-bandwidth, low-latency environments. For this, understanding 5G and further technology infrastructure and its applications will be necessary.

e. High Priority for Cybersecurity:

- Trend: As cyber vulnerability and threats become more sophisticated, cybersecurity will remain a top priority for organizations.

- Impact: The demand for cybersecurity professionals, ethical hackers, and security architects will increase. The professionals will be required to stay updated on the latest security threats and technologies as crucial needs.

f. Integration of Blockchain Technology:

- Trend: The Blockchain will be used beyond cryptocurrencies, in many domain areas, like applications in supply chain management, healthcare, and finance.

- Impact: The careers in blockchain development, security, and project management will rise. The Professionals will be required to understand decentralized networks, smart contracts, and cryptographic principles, for the implementation.

g. Rise of Green IT and Sustainability:

- Trend: There will be a growing focus on reducing the environmental impact of IT operations with Green IT practices.

- Impact: The roles of sustainability officers, green IT specialists, and energy-efficient systems designers will increase. The understanding of sustainable practices and technologies will become mandatory.

h. Adoption of Remote and Hybrid Work Models:

- Trend: Post-covid, the Remote and Hybrid work models are becoming more prevalent. This requires high-end collaboration and productivity tools.

- Impact: The IT professionals will require expertise in remote work technologies, virtual collaboration tools, and cybersecurity measures to support distributed teams.

Forecasting Future Career Opportunities

The evolving technologies in the IT industry would change future career trends. The opportunities would radically change as well. We will have to keep an eye on these possible future opportunities and look for the skills and readiness required as mature IT professionals.

a. AI and Machine Learning Engineers:

- Role: The job will be for the Development and deployment of AI models and machine learning algorithms.

- Skills Needed: Proficiency in programming languages, especially Python, the know-how of AI frameworks (TensorFlow, PyTorch), and adequate skills in data analysis and algorithm development.

b. Quantum Computing Specialists:

- Role: The job will be for Research and development for quantum algorithms and applications.

- Skills Needed: Knowledge of quantum mechanics, experience with quantum programming languages (Qiskit, Cirq), and awareness of quantum hardware will be expected.

c. IoT and Edge Computing Experts:

- Role: The expectation for the job will be to Design and implement IoT systems and edge computing solutions.

- Skills Needed: Familiarity with IoT platforms, sensor integration, real-time data processing, and edge computing architectures will be required.

d. 5G Network Engineers and Application Developers:

- Role: The requirement will be to Build and maintain 5G networks and develop applications leveraging 5G capabilities.

- Skills Needed: The knowledge of 5G infrastructure, network management, and application development for high-bandwidth, low-latency environments will be expected.

e. Cybersecurity Professionals:

- Role: The responsibility will be to Protect systems and data from cyber threats.

- Skills Needed: Expertise in network security, ethical hacking, incident response, and knowledge of security frameworks and regulations will be required.

f. Blockchain - Developers and Project Managers:

- Role: It's required to Develop and manage blockchain-based applications and projects.

- Skills Needed: The understanding of blockchain technologies, smart contract development, and project management skills will become mandatory.

g. Green IT and Sustainability Specialists:

- Role: The R&R will be to implement sustainable IT practices and technologies.

- Skills Needed: Knowledge of energy-efficient systems, green IT best practices, and environmental impact assessment will be required.

h. Remote Work Technology Experts:

- Role: Support and enhance remote work infrastructure and tools will be required

- Skills Needed: Proficiency in remote collaboration tools, virtual desktop infrastructure (VDI), and cybersecurity for remote work environments will become mandatory.

Preparing for Future Career Opportunities

As we have seen the futuristic job opportunities, you should also seek to get ready for these upcoming opportunities. We shall quickly look at the pointers for the readiness needed.

a. Continuous Learning and Skill Development:

- The IT Professional should engage in lifelong learning through online courses, certifications, and attending industry conferences.

- You should stay updated on emerging technologies and trends by following industry news, blogs, and publications.

b. Networking and Professional Associations:

- You can join professional associations and online communities to network with peers and industry leaders.

- You should explore participating in forums, webinars, and local meetups to share knowledge and stay informed.

c. Practical Experience and Exploration:

- The IT Professional should gain hands-on experience with new technologies through sandbox projects, internships, and collaborative work.

- You should explore emerging technologies to understand their practical applications and limitations.

d. Cross-Disciplinary Skills:

- Enhance versatility with the development of skills in adjacent fields such as data science, cybersecurity, and business management.

- You should understand the broader implications of technology on business and society.

e. Soft Skills Development:

- Focus on developing soft skills such as communication, leadership, problem-solving, and adaptability.

- These skills will be highly valuable in collaborative and dynamic work environments.

Conclusion

IT professionals can advance their careers in the rapidly evolving technology landscape by studying trends and actively developing relevant skills. They should assess market trends alongside forecasts and prepare themselves for upcoming changes.

Chapter 11

Wrap up with Case Studies and Success Stories

While we keep an eye on the Skills and Trends in the IT Industry, we must go through some of the case studies and success stories, to understand it well. Here we will explore the skills, technology and people transformation, to understand more with practical and live examples.

Case Study: Skills Transformation

Organizational Digital Credentials Programs for Employee Career Development

Rapid changes are occurring in IT technology alongside various industry trends. It has become essential for IT companies to invest in employee training focused on the latest business-oriented technologies. This investment allows organizations to remain competitive and achieve their growth objectives. However, organizational goals must align with the aspirations of employees. Additionally, while employees pursue training and certifications, these efforts should be aligned with actual business requirements.

- Advantages of Organizational Goals oriented Digital Credentials

  a. **Productivity Enhancement:** The training programs are designed and implemented according to the organization's business needs. As a result, employees gain in-depth knowledge and skills related to the necessary technologies, tools, and techniques. This enhances their delivery capabilities, leading to improved performance and increased productivity among the trained employees.

  b. **Right Skilled Staffing:** By aligning training plans with organizational business requirements, a pool of appropriately skilled staff is created. This alignment facilitates the recruitment of individuals with the specific skills needed for various positions. Consequently, project delivery becomes more efficient. Additionally, it allows for a more effective allocation of the budget spent on training relative to the desired project outcomes, ensuring cost-effectiveness.

  c. **Higher Employee Engagement:** By considering the aspirations of employees during training, they become motivated and engage more effectively with larger organizational goals. This leads to increased commitment and improved work delivery, ultimately achieving higher employee satisfaction.

  d. **Talent Retention:** The investment in training leads to employees seeing a clear career path associated with their development. As a result, they pursue job roles and opportunities that align with their skills, which significantly improves retention, particularly in niche areas.

- Approaches for Digital Credentials Programs

  a. **Monthly / Quarterly training programs:** Service lines across various skill domains can offer monthly and quarterly training and certification programs. This enables employees to allocate time for learning while managing their project responsibilities. Additionally, project-specific training can be arranged as needed.

b. **Digital Credentials Initiatives:** For various areas, such as platforms, technical and project management, leadership, and process and methodology, certifications and badges should align with larger organizational objectives.

c. **Target and reward plans:** The organization can set training and certification goals based on business needs. A recognition and reward mechanism can be established to motivate employees to achieve the required certifications within a specified timeframe.

- Pitfalls of unplanned Organizational training

a. **Excess Skill Capacity:** As business conditions continue to fluctuate, the need for individuals with specific skills and perspectives can change dramatically. This may lead to excess capacity in certain skill areas, creating an undesirable situation for both the organization and its employees.

b. **Employee motivation loss:** If employees are trained and certified in specific skills and platforms, and later do not utilize this knowledge promptly, they tend to forget it. This can also lead to demotivation among employees.

Conclusion

To achieve business success while fostering continuous learning and skill growth among employees, it is essential to define effective training and certification plans. This involves balancing the organization's needs with employees' skills and aspirations. Organizational digital credential programs should be thoughtfully planned and executed to align with business objectives. Implementing Reskill and Upskill programs to develop the right skills and deploy skilled individuals promptly creates an ideal situation that benefits both the organization and its employees.

Case Study: Technology Transformation - Netflix

Netflix's Cloud Journey on AWS

- **Netflix** is one of the world's leading entertainment services with over 260 million members in more than 190 countries. Netflix uses AWS for nearly all its computing and storage needs, including databases, analytics, recommendation engines, video transcoding, and more—hundreds of functions that in total use more than 100,000 server instances on AWS.

- **Adopting AWS:** How Netflix began its cloud journey. A three-day outage in 2008 unveiled an imminent capacity crunch for Netflix. It was also struggling with scaling issues on its legacy architecture. It needed a solution that did not limit them to vertical scaling. It wanted to scale horizontally, have reliable uptime, and keep cloud spend cost-effective. Netflix was prompted to explore cloud service providers and ultimately chose AWS. At first, Netflix adopted Amazon EC2 and Amazon S3 for foundational computing and storage services. The company then steadily expanded its migration to AWS, starting with front-end applications before migrating its databases from Oracle, along with other backend infrastructure.

- **AWS Infrastructure:** AWS provides Netflix with computing, storage, and infrastructure that allows the company to scale quickly, operate securely, and meet capacity needs anywhere in the world. Moreover, Netflix, a leading content producer, has used AWS to build a studio in the cloud. This virtual studio enables Netflix to engage top artistic talent, no matter the location, and Netflix artists and partners have the freedom to collaborate without technological or geographical barriers.

  Now, Netflix is all-in on AWS, supporting its more than 100 million customers with a fully cloud-based architecture and no longer managing its data centres.

- **Auto-Scaling:** Netflix has seen resurgent higher viewing and increased member growth during certain periods. To meet this demand, the control plane services of Netflix needed to scale very quickly. The technological collaboration was achieved with AWS to meet capacity needs in computing, and storage, as well as provide the necessary infrastructure, with AWS Auto Scaling.

- **Automating security:** Netflix uses AWS Lambda to automatically validate new instances and trigger shutdowns for unauthorized instances. Netflix also works with AWS to meet regulatory requirements and protect data. Cybersecurity is achieved with multi-factor authentication, CloudTrail, and ConsoleMe among others.

The business with technology collaboration between Netflix and AWS is a sheer example of a successful mega-partnership between them, to serve the entertainment services across the globe.

[reference: Amazon Web Services (AWS)- https://aws.amazon.com/solutions/case-studies/netflix-case-study/

Netflix and AWS are Registered trademarks of the respective organizations.]

Case Study: Technology Transformation - IBM

IBM watsonx Gen AI: Expertise on Call

- **Healthcare:** To differentiate themselves in what is both a complex and crucially important space, healthcare and insurance companies need to continuously innovate to improve customer service and retention. Consumers expect to receive quick and accurate answers to their queries wherever and whenever they want.

- **Humana:** One of the largest insurance providers in the US, Humana offers Medicare supplements, health insurance, dental insurance, vision insurance and pharmacy coverage to more than 13 million customers across the country. Humana chose to work with IBM Watson®, the industry leader in enterprise AI and began a collaboration with IBM. The solution combines multiple Watson applications in a single conversational assistant and runs on IBM Cloud˚, while the watsonx™ Assistant for Voice runs on premises at Humana.

- **watsonx in a nutshell:** The solution components used for this specific use case scenario were as below:

  a. IBM watsonx Assistant: Conversational AI for fast and friendly customer care-

  The IBM watsonx Assistant is a next-gen conversational AI solution that empowers anyone in the organization to effortlessly build generative AI Assistants that deliver frictionless self-service experiences to customers across any device or channel, help boost employee productivity, and scale across your business.

  b. IBM Cloud: An enterprise cloud platform designed for even the most regulated industries, delivering a highly resilient, performant, secure and compliant cloud.

  c. IBM watson: Through advancements in core watson technologies, IBM has developed the next-generation AI and data platform and set of AI assistants with watsonx.

  Humana's Voice Agent with Watson provides a faster, friendlier and more consistent way for administrative staff at healthcare providers to access pre-service, medical eligibility, verification, authorization and referral information without the need to speak with a live agent. The solution relies on AI to understand the intent of a provider's call, verify they are permitted to access the system and member information, and then determine how best to provide the information requested.

- **Reflection:** Humana reduced the costly pre-service calls and improved the user experience with conversational Artificial Intelligence. The solution receives more than 7,000 voice calls from 120 providers per business day, and feedback from users has been incredibly positive.

  [Reference: IBM - https://www.ibm.com/case-studies/humana

IBM, the IBM logo, ibm.com, IBM Cloud, IBM Watson, and With Watson are trademarks or registered trademarks of International Business Machines Corporation, in the United States and/or other countries.]

Profiles of Successful IT Professionals:

We shall go through the high-profile successful IT Professionals, to understand their career path and success journey.

N. R. Narayana Murthy - Indian entrepreneur

Mr Narayana Murthy is one of the prominent pioneers, 'Maha-Guru' of IT Industry in India.

- **Education:** Mr Narayana Murthy went to the National Institute of Engineering and graduated in 1967 with a bachelor's degree in electrical engineering. In 1969 he received his master's degree from the Indian Institute of Technology, Kanpur. In 2007, Mr Murthy received an honorary degree from Lancaster University.

- **Career:** Mr Murthy first worked as a research associate under a faculty at IIM Ahmedabad and then later as the chief systems programmer. There he worked on India's first time-sharing computer system and designed and implemented a BASIC interpreter for Electronics Corporation of India Limited. He started a company named 'Softronics'. When that company failed after about a year and a half, he joined Patni Computer Systems in Pune.

- **Infosys:** He founded Infosys in 1981 and was the CEO from 1981 to 2002, as well as the chairman from 2002 to 2011. In 2011, he stepped down from the board and became the chairman emeritus. In June 2013, Mr Murthy was appointed as the executive chairman for five years. He has now retired and taken the title of chairman emeritus.

- **Life Achievements:** Mr Murthy has been listed among the 12 greatest entrepreneurs of our time by Fortune magazine. He has been described as the "Father of the Indian IT sector" by Time magazine and CNBC for his contribution to outsourcing in India. In 2005, he co-chaired the World Economic Forum in Davos, Switzerland. He has also written several books, including A Better India: A Better World and A Clear Blue Sky: Stories and Poems on Conflict and Hope. Mr Murthy has received several awards and has been honoured by the Indian Government with the Padma Shri and Padma Vibhushan awards.

Sundar Pichai – CEO of Google

Mr Pichai Sundararajan, better known as Sundar Pichai, is an Indian-born American business executive. He is the chief executive officer of Alphabet Inc. and its subsidiary Google. Mr Pichai was born in Madurai, Tamil Nadu, India, to a Tamil Brahmin family.

- **Education:** Mr Pichai earned his degree from IIT Kharagpur in metallurgical engineering and is a distinguished alumnus of that institution. He holds an M.S. from Stanford University in materials science and engineering, and an MBA from the Wharton School of the University of Pennsylvania, where he was named a Siebel Scholar and a Palmer Scholar, respectively.

- **Career:** Mr Pichai began his career as a materials engineer. He had a short stint at the management consulting firm McKinsey & Co.

- **Google:** Mr Pichai joined Google in 2004, where he led the product management and innovation efforts for a suite of Google's client software products, including Google Chrome and ChromeOS, as well as being responsible for Google Drive. In addition, he went on to oversee the development of other applications such as Gmail and Google Maps. In 2010, Mr Pichai also announced the open-sourcing of the new video codec VP8 by Google and introduced the new video format, WebM. The Chromebook was released in 2012. In 2013, Mr Pichai added Android to the list of Google products that he oversaw.

- Mr Pichai was selected to become the next CEO of Google on August 10, 2015, after previously being appointed chief product officer by then-CEO Larry Page. On October 24, 2015, he stepped into the new position after the formation of Alphabet Inc., the new holding company for the Google company family. He was appointed to the Alphabet Board of Directors in 2017.

- **Life Achievements:** Mr Pichai was included in Time's annual list of the 100 most influential people in 2016 and 2020. He was also included in the Time 100 AI list in 2024. In 2022, Mr Pichai received the Padma Bhushan in the category of Trade and Industry from the Government of India.

Mr Narayana Murthy and Mr Sundar Pichai are highly inspiring personalities and have achieved tremendous success in their IT career. Both have exceptional skills and unwavering dedication to achieving their career results. They are role models among others to study the life and career journey. We should take cues from them for our self-development.

Lessons Learned from Industry Leaders

We shall study the Lessons Learned from Industry Leaders and adopt them for our progress. You would see how the personalities of individuals have exemplified successful leaders. It is worth learning from them, imbibing their principles and actions, putting up a plan for us, and abiding by it for our betterment.

Adaptability and Agility

- Satya Nadella (Microsoft): Nadella was instrumental in transforming Microsoft into a more agile and innovative company by studying the IT market and focusing on cloud computing.

- Marc Benioff (Salesforce): Founder of cloud-based CRM, Benioff emphasizes the importance of quick responses to technological advancements.

Lessons: Swiftly adopt change with new technologies and market trends. Agility should be built.

Customer-Centric Approach

- Jeff Bezos (Amazon): Bezos transformed Amazon with a relentless focus on client experience, which has resulted in the company's enormous growth.

- Jesper Brodin (Ikea): Since Brodin took over in 2017, the company underwent a drastic transformation. He emphasized exceptional customer service, proving that a strong customer-centric culture can differentiate a company in competitive markets.

Lessons: Prioritize customer satisfaction and user experience to create long-term client value.

Continuous Learning and Innovation

- Elon Musk (SpaceX, Tesla): Musk's success is ascribed to his aggressive innovative mindset, constantly pushing the boundaries of technology, and seeking continuous learning.

- Sundar Pichai (Google/Alphabet): Pichai supports a culture of result-oriented innovation, leading to the development of pioneering products.

Lessons: Foster a culture of continuous learning and encourage innovative thinking. Invest in Research and Development and support creative problem-solving within your teams.

Visionary Leadership

- Steve Jobs (Apple): Apple's products revolutionized the technology industry with visionary leadership by Steve.

- Jack Ma (Alibaba): Jack Ma's visionary approach helped Alibaba to become a global e-commerce giant.

Lessons: Set a clear vision and channel your organizational efforts with the vision. Inspire the organization team to pursue it passionately.

Resilience and Perseverance

- Reed Hastings (Netflix): Hastings demonstrated resilience by pivoting Netflix to be a content streaming service. He explored and implemented a business culture called "Freedom and Responsibility", which resulted in high resilience by the organizational team.

- Linus Torvalds (Linux): Torvalds' perseverance led to the widespread adoption of Linux, despite numerous challenges that were faced at the organization level.

Lessons: Remain dedicated to your goals, even when facing constant obstacles. As well, as remain prepared to pivot and stay resilient to face the challenges.

Key Takeaways from IT Experts

We will have a summarized look for the key takeaways, that we can learn from the IT Experts and adopt in our day-to-day life for our progress.

Embrace Emerging Technologies

- Takeaway: Stay tuned to the latest technological advancements and adopt them to integrate these into your projects. The latest technologies like Gen AI, blockchain, cloud and quantum computing are continuously evolving and can offer substantial competitive advantages.

Promote Collaborative Culture

- Takeaway: Foster a collaborative work environment where team members are empowered to generate and share new ideas and work together on innovative solutions. The collaboration often leads to more effective problem-solving and creative thinking.

Focus on Cybersecurity

- Takeaway: With the rapidly increasing vulnerability and cyber threats, it is critical to implement robust cybersecurity measures. Review and upgrade the security protocols regularly, educate employees on security practices and invest in and adopt advanced security technologies.

Utilize Data-Driven Decision Making

- Takeaway: Informed Decision making and business risk-taking are leading to the adoption of DDDM. You should leverage the data analytics for your decisions. The consolidation and analysis of large-volume data can provide valuable insights into customer behaviour, market trends, and operational efficiencies. This would help to make more calculated and strategic decisions.

Prioritize Talent Development

- Takeaway: Continuous learning and development are essential for remaining relevant and competitive. You should motivate your team to pursue business-required education, certifications, and training programs to keep their skills latest and relevant.

Agile Methodologies

- Takeaway: Implement agile methodologies to improve project management and delivery. With the squad and Tribe formation, the teams are empowered to make the decisions and speed up delivery. Agile practices help teams to respond more quickly to changes, improve collaboration, and deliver better results.

Sustainable Practices

- Takeaway: You should incorporate sustainable practices in IT delivery operations. This can include optimizing energy usage, reducing e-waste, and promoting eco-friendly initiatives. Sustainability helps the environment and enhances the company's reputation with Go-Green initiatives.

Conclusion

The lessons learned from industry leaders and insights from IT experts emphasize the importance of adaptability, client focus, continuous learning, and innovation. By incorporating these principles into their professional practices, IT professionals can enhance their effectiveness, drive technological advancements, and make significant contributions to their organizations' success. It is often more beneficial to learn from the experiences of leaders rather than by making our own mistakes.

Final Thoughts on Building a Successful IT Career

In the final section, we will summarize the thought process behind building a successful IT career. Essentially, it's a combination of our actions, the knowledge we acquire, how we apply what we learn, the practices we adopt, the guidance we seek and receive, the opportunities we choose at the right moments, and the experiences we gain along the way. When we integrate all of these elements, it transforms into a successful life story.

Adopt Constant Learning

- Stay Current and Relevant: The IT industry is evolving very rapidly. Tune yourself to the latest technologies, market trends, and best practices. Enhance your expertise and increase your market value.

- Enhance Skills: Utilize various avenues like training, and certifications, and participate in industrial conferences, and webinars to stay up to date.

Soft Skills are Equally Important

- Communication: Effective communication is crucial. The speaking, listening, body language is very important. The presentation skill is another niche area, you should vouch for. Take up some professional training on how to present, and how to make expressions with stakeholders. It pays off. The clear and concise communication is key to success.

- Leadership and Collaboration: The Leadership is about inspiring and motivating stakeholders and people that you collaborate. It could be team people or peers, colleagues, and outside the organization. You should cultivate leadership qualities and collaboration with all that you interact with.

Network and Develop Relationships

- Professional Networks: Join professional Institutes, and organizations, attend industry conferences, and participate in various forums. Networking can provide leads for opportunities. You could gain valuable insights from peers and mentors.

- Mentorship: Engage with proficient mentors who can guide and support. Also, provide giveback by mentoring others to share your knowledge and experience, contributing to the growth of the organization and overall IT community.

Change is Only Constant

- Embrace Change: As we have seen, the IT industry is very dynamic. Being adaptable and adopting the change will help you navigate new challenges and seize emerging opportunities.

- Develop an Analytical mind: Looking at things with different views helps to build an analytical mindset. The analytical mind helps in problem-solving, which is valued highly in the industry.

Innovation that matters

- Hone up Creativity: Innovation often involves thinking outside the box. Always remain open-minded and propose new ideas and solutions.

- Continuous Improvement: Strive for continuous improvement in your work processes and technologies. Small steps make big leaps. Develop Atomic Habits. With tiny changes, you could achieve remarkable results over time.

Prioritize Work-Life Balance

- Conquer Stress: IT careers are becoming over-demanding. The fatigue and stress should not override you. Ensure you have strategies in place to manage stress and avoid burnout. Make a habit of planning regular breaks and exercise. Develop hobbies, that can help maintain a healthy work-life balance.

- Personal Growth: Investing in personal development is very much required. The so-called non-technical skills like time management, goal setting, and self-discipline are crucial for a balanced and successful career. Become a Project Manager of your own life and career; and drive yourself to success!!

Encouragement and Motivation for Readers

Once you are in the career flow, and especially in the IT field, advancing in the career is both exciting and challenging. I would note some tricks and tips for you, as encouragement and motivation, that you could imbibe.

Trust and Believe in Yourself

- Confidence: Impress your subconscious mind with success. It will do miracles for you. Trust in your abilities and knowledge. The confidence in your skills will help you tackle challenges and seize opportunities.

- Growth Mindset: Think and Grow Rich - Author **Napoleon Hill** said – "Whatever the mind can conceive and believe, it can achieve". Embrace a growth mindset. Look at challenges as opportunities to learn and grow, rather than hurdles. That's the Law of success.

Maintain Curiosity and Passion

- Curiosity: Start with Why. Curiosity drives innovation. People don't buy WHAT you do, they buy WHY you do it. Always maintain a sense of curiosity. The desire to explore, ask questions, and seek answers will lead you to discoveries and innovations.

- Passion: Create deep passion to raise your skills, that will lead to success. Let your passion drive you to reach higher goals. The passion fuels perseverance and resilience, which are essential for sustaining the success.

Endure Through Challenges

- Resilience: Every professional has his ups and downs in their career. What is needed is to bounce back from setbacks and keep moving forward, taking lessons learned and proactive measures to avoid them in future.

- Persistence: Difficulties come and go. One must keep going. It's like riding the waves in the sea. You should ride it one after the other. It requires persistence to achieve it. Put in the effort and persist through difficulties.

Create Positive Impression

- Contribution: Target to make a positive impact through your collaboration and work. Whether it's enhancing processes, developing innovative solutions, or helping others, your involvement matters.

- Inspire Others: Giving back to the community or organization is necessary. You could motivate your peers and juniors. Remain open-minded to share your experiences, and mentor aspiring IT professionals. This will help inspire the people.

Celebrate Your Achievements

- Recognize Success: Appreciation for small things matters the most. Learn to appreciate yourself as well. Take time to share and celebrate your achievements. Recognizing your progress boosts motivation and morale.

- Reflect and Learn: Look back on your endeavours, both successes and failures. Every experience gives valuable lessons that contribute to your growth.

Enjoy the Career as a Journey You Like the Most

- Balance: Devote time to your family. Always maintain a healthy balance between your professional and personal life. The success is holistic and includes happiness and well-being.

- Fulfilment: Enjoy your work passionately. Your career could lead to reaching a high goal or position, that would be your destination, though the journey to reach there as well is valuable. Enjoy it!!

Conclusion

By embracing these final thoughts, you can maintain your motivation. Remember, your career is a journey, not a destination. Enjoy every step along the way. The key to success is to love what you do and do what you love. Your education serves as a foundation, while your career is the masterpiece you create. You can build a successful and fulfilling career in the IT industry. Keep in mind that the journey is just as important as the destination. Stay passionate and continue learning. Focus on personal and professional growth by enhancing your skills, which will increase your market value. Your dedication and hard work will guide you toward an amazing career in the ever-evolving field of technology.

Wishing you all the best on your enjoyable journey in the IT career!

Explore the Mind Maps!!

- ## Building a Successful IT Career – Your Steps

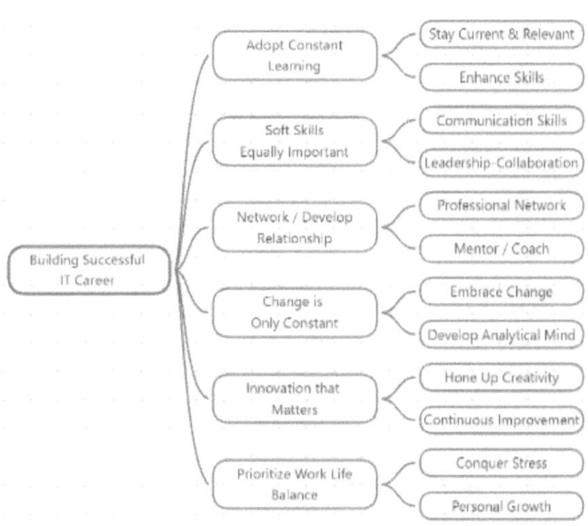

- ## Encouragement and Motivation for You

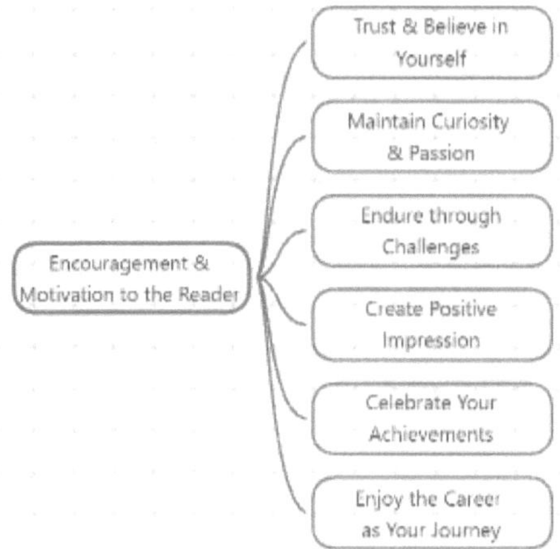

Annexure

A] Overview of IT Industries and Services:

There are various Commercial Industries that are supported by the IT Industry and form the client pool for the organizations. The Sector Management Structure in the IT Industry is formed considering the client Industry. Noting it as a reference to understand the Big Picture!

Industries

Industry	Brief Description
Banking	All the Government / Public Sector and Private Banks
Capital Markets	Organizations that are marketplaces for buying and selling bonds, stocks, currencies and other financial assets
Insurance	Companies that offer risk management in the form of insurance contracts
Distribution	Major part of the supply chain, connecting manufacturers and suppliers with consumers, businesses, and institutions

Industry	Brief Description
Communications, Media, and Information Services	Companies that provide communication services using fixed-line networks or those that provide wireless access and Media / Information services
Education	Organizations and businesses that provide products and services aimed at enhancing the quality of education in society
Energy, Resources, and Utilities	Companies that generate, transmit, and distribute natural resources like electricity, natural gas, and water
Healthcare	Organizations and services that provide medical care and support to individuals
Life Sciences	Companies operating in the fields of pharmaceuticals, biotechnology, medical devices, biomedical technologies, nutraceuticals, cosmeceuticals, food processing
Manufacturing	Companies doing production of goods on a large scale, utilizing various processes and technologies to transform raw materials into finished products
Public Services	All Governmental services for the public
Retail	Business of selling goods and services to consumers for personal use
Travel and Transportation	Companies that deal with the movement of people and products – e.g. airlines, trucking, railroads, shipping, and logistics firms, providing transportation infrastructure

Services

These typically form the Service Lines in the Matrix structured IT organizations.

Services	Brief Description
Artificial Intelligence	Services that analyse production data to identify inefficiencies and optimize manufacturing processes, without human actions
Cloud Platforms	AWS, Azure, Google, IBM, Hybrid Cloud platforms – support & services
Cognitive Business Operations	Processes and decisions that can sense, respond, and learn
Consulting	Service that helps clients use information technology (IT) to achieve their business goals
Cybersecurity	Practice of protecting an organization's IT infrastructure from cyber threats
Data and Analytics	Process of using data to improve business outcomes, processes, and decisions
Enterprise Solutions	Integration of multiple facets of a company's business
IoT and Digital Engineering	Support to businesses improve their digital strategies and create new opportunities for innovation.
Sustainability Services	Services involve collaborating with clients and the ecosystem to create new IT products or services that help an organization achieve its sustainability goals.

Services	Brief Description
Network Solutions and Services	Support applications at the network application layer that connects users working in offices, branches, or remote locations to applications and data in a network;

B] Reference Templates

Please refer to the templates and use them for your skills planning and tracking, referred to earlier in various chapters.

1) Skill Gap Analysis

SKILL/COMPETENCY	Skill Description	Skill Importance	Skill Level Required
Skill 1			
Skill 2			
Skill 3			
Skill 4			
Skill 5			
Skill 6			
Skill 7			
Skill 8			
Skill 9			
Skill 10			

Skill Importance Levels	
Rating	**Meaning**
1	**Not Important:** 'Nice-to-have', although not essential.
2	**Minor Importance:** Occasionally useful, but not used much.
3	**Moderately Important:** Regularly used; Required for the current role.
4	**Very Important:** Frequently used; Not having will constrain work. Important to have.
5	**Critically Important:** Must for primary responsibilities and the job.
Skill Level Requirements	
Rating	**Meaning**
1	**New:** Limited exposure to the skill, at the learning stage. Requires significant guidance.
2	**Basic:** foundational knowledge, may not have hands-on. Can do simple tasks with guidance.
3	**Experienced:** Can perform tasks independently; require some guidance for complex work.
4	**Expert:** Deep knowledge, high hands-on experience. Can handle any complex ToDo's
5	**Thought Leader:** Master of the skill. Recognized as a go-to person. Can guide/train others.

2) SWOT Analysis

SW/OT	**Opportunities** (External, Positive)	**Threats** (External, Negative)
Strengths (internal, Positive)	**Strength-Opportunity strategy** Which strength of yours can be used to maximize the Opportunity identified?	**Strength-Threats strategies** How can you use your strength to minimise the threats you identified?
Weaknesses (Internal, Negative)	**Weakness-Opportunity strategy:** What actions can you take to minimise your weaknesses using the opportunity identified?	**Weakness-Threats strategies** How can you minimise your weakness to avoid the threats you identified?

3) Individual Development Plan (IDP)

Name		Current Position	Organisation / Project Name
Role		Band	Reviewer

Short Term Goal		Long Term Goal

Skill Upgrade Plan	Source	Plan Start	Plan End	Actual Start	Actual End	Status

Development Activities to Achieve the Skill Upgrade Plan						
Task/ Objective	Assignment	Plan Start	Plan End	Actual Start	Actual End	Status

4) Task Prioritization – the Eisenhower Matrix – Customised to your needs

	Urgent	Not Urgent
Important	**Do** Tasks with Defined Deadlines and high Consequences	**Schedule** Tasks with undefined deadlines having long-term goals
Not Important	**Delegate** Tasks that must be done, but do not require your specific skills and time.	**Delete** Distractions and unnecessary tasks, Wastage of Time and effort

5) Curriculum Vitae (CV)

	Your Name **Your Country** **Phone:** **Email:**
Education • Your Educational Qualification – Degree / Year **Digital Credentials** • Your Technical and PM Certifications, Badges **Languages** • The fluency for Languages you can read/speak well (High / Medium/Low)	**Profile** • High-Level Profile Summary, depicting your experience **Key skills** • The Important skills you have **Technical skills:** • The technical Languages you are well versed with **Soft Skills:** • Any Specifics about Presentation Skills, Public speaking **Tools:** • The Development and management-related tools **Key courses and training** • Important Training and courses you have completed

<table>
<tr><td></td><td>

Work experience

- A high-level work experience summary of your respective role/s.

Assignment history

- The Delivery Role Assignments and Achievements – List with Chronological descending order.

Additional information

- Your Membership with Industrial Institutes etc
- Your Organizational Contributions etc
- Your Hobbies

</td></tr>
</table>

C] Glossary of IT Terms and Acronyms

Acronym	Description
ACP	Agile Certified Practitioner
AI	Artificial Intelligence
AWS	Amazon Web Services
CCPA	California Consumer Privacy Act
CDO	Chief Data Officer
CEO	Chief Executive Officer
CI/CD	Continuous Integration/Continuous Delivery
CSM	Certified Scrum Master
CSPO	Certified Scrum Product Owner

Acronym	Description
CTO	Chief Technology Officer
DASSM	Disciplined Agile Senior Scrum Master
DDDM	Data-Driven Decision Making
DDoS	Distributed Denial of Service
EDA	Exploratory Data Analysis
ELK	Elasticsearch, Logstash, and Kibana
GCP	Google Cloud Platform
GDPR	General Data Protection Regulation – EU law
HIPAA	Health Insurance Portability and Accountability Act
IaC	Infrastructure as Code
IBV	IBM Business Value
IDE	Integrated Development Environment
IDP	Individual Development Plan
IoT	Internet of Things
ISTQB	International Software Testing Qualifications Board
IT	Information Technology
ITIL	Information Technology Infrastructure Library
JVM	Java Virtual Machine
ML	Machine Learning
MOOC	Massive open online course
OCJP	Oracle Certified Professional Java Programmer
PM	Project Manager
PMBOK	Project Management Body of Knowledge

Acronym	Description
PMI	Project Management Institute
PMI PMP	Project Management Professional Certification
PO	Product Owner
PoLP	Principle of Least Privilege
QA	Quality Assurance
RDS	Relational Database Service
SLO	Service Level Objectives
SRE	Site Reliability Engineers
UIDAI	Unique Identification Authority of India
WCAG	Web Content Accessibility Guidelines

D] References

Site	URL
ACM Digital Library	https://dl.acm.org
Alibaba	https://Alibaba.com
Angular	https://angular.dev
Ansible	https://www.ansible.com
Apache Hadoop	https://hadoop.apache.org
Apache JMeter	https://jmeter.apache.org
Apache Kafka	https://kafka.apache.org
Appian RPA	https://appian.com
Appium	https://appium.io
Apple	https://www.apple.com
Ars Technica	https://arstechnica.com

Site	URL
ASP.NET	https://www.asp.net
Association for Computing Machinery	https://www.acm.org
Automation Anywhere	https://www.automationanywhere.com
AWS Amazon	aws.amazon.com
AWS Case Study for Netflix	https://aws.amazon.com/solutions/case-studies/netflix-case-study
Bash	https://www.gnu.org/software/bash/
Behance	https://www.behance.net
Blockchain	https://www.blockchain.com
Blue Prism	https://www.blueprism.com
Case Study-Netflix	https://aws.amazon.com/solutions/case-studies/netflix/
Cassandra	https://cassandra.apache.org
ChatGPT	https://chatgpt.com/
CircleCI	https://circleci.com
Cisco	https://www.cisco.com
CoAP	https://coap.space
CompTIA Network	https://www.comptia.org
Coursera	https://www.coursera.org/in
Devpost	https://devpost.com
Django	https://www.djangoproject.com
Docker	https://www.docker.com
Dribbble	https://dribbble.com

Site	URL
EC-Council	https://www.eccouncil.org
edX	https://www.edx.org
Ethereum	https://ethereum.com
Facebook	https://www.facebook.com
Flask	https://flask.palletsprojects.com
Gartner	https://www.gartner.com
GitHub	https://github.com/
Glassdoor	https://www.Glassdoor.com
Google Cloud	https://cloud.google.com/
Google/Alphabet	https://www.google.com/
Grafana	https://grafana.com
Gulp	https://gulpjs.com
Hackaday	https://hackaday.com
HackerEarth	https://www.hackerearth.com
Hackers News	https://news.ycombinator.com
Hyperledger	https://www.hyperledger.org
IBM	https://www.ibm.com
IBM Case Study for Humana	https://www.ibm.com/case-studies/humana
IBM Cloud	https://www.ibm.com/cloud
IBM RPA	https://www.ibm.com/products/robotic-process-automation
IEEE	https://www.ieee.org
Ikea	https://www.ikea.com

Site	URL
Indeed	https://www.Indeed.com
InfoQ	https://www.infoq.com
Informatica	https://www.informatica.com
Information Systems Security (CISSP)	https://www.isc2.org
Infosys	https://www.infosys.com
Institute for Certification of Computing Professionals (ICCP) for CDP	https://onlinecourses.iccp.org
Internshala	https://www.Internshala.com
ISACA	https://www.isaca.org
ISC2	https://www.isc2.org
ISTQB	https://www.istqb.org
ITIL	https://www.itilcertificationcourses.com
Java	https://www.oracle.com/in/java/
Jenkins	https://www.jenkins.io
Jira	https://www.atlassian.com
Journal of Information Technology (Sage Journals)	https://journals.sagepub.com/home
Keras	https://keras.io
Krebs on Security	https://krebsonsecurity.com
Kubernetes	https://kubernetes.io

Site	URL
LamdaTest	https://www.iamdatest.com
LinkedIn	https://in.linkedin.com
Linux	https://www.linux.org
Meet up	https://www.meetup.com
Microsoft	https://www.microsoft.com
Microsoft Azure	https://azure.microsoft.com/en-us/
Microsoft Teams	https://www.microsoft.com/en-in/microsoft-teams/group-chat-software
MongoDB	https://www.mongodb.com
MQTT	https://mqtt.org
MySQL	https://www.mysql.com
Netflix	https://www.netflix.com
Node.js	https://nodejs.org
Npm	https://npmjs.com
NumPy	https://numpy.org
Open Group	https://www.opengroup.org
Oracle	https://www.oracle.com
Pandas	https://pandas.pydata.org
Pinterest	https://in.pinterest.com
Pluralsight	https://www.pluralsight.com
PostgreSQL	https://www.postgresql.org
Prometheus	https://www.prometheus.io
Python	https://www.python.org/

Site	URL
PyTorch	https://pytorch.org
React	https://react.dev
React Native	https://reactnative.dev
Reddit	https://reddit.com
Salesforce	https://www.salesforce.com
Scikit-learn	https://www.scikit-learn.org
Scrum Alliance (CSM, CSPO)	https://www.scrumalliance.org
Selenium	https://www.selenium.dev
Slack	https://slack.com
Snowflake	https://www.snowflake.com
Solidity	https://soliditylang.org
SpaceX	https://www.spacex.com
Spring	https://spring.io
Stack Overflow	https://stackoverflow.com
Tableau	https://www.tableau.com
Talend	https://www.talend.com
TCS	https://www.tcs.com
TechCrunch	https://techcrunch.com
TensorFlow	https://www.tensorflow.org
Terraform	https://www.terraform.io
Tesla	https://www.tesla.com
Trello	https://www.trello.com

Site	URL
Tricentis Tosca	https://www.tricentis.com
Twitter / X	https://X.com
Udemy	http://www.udemy.com
UiPath	https://www.uipath.com
Unity	https://unity.com
Vue.js	https://vuejs.org
Webpack	https://webpack.js.org
Wikipedia	https://en.wikipedia.org/wiki/India
Yarn	https://yarnpkg.com
Zoom	https://zoom.us

Acknowledgements

It gives me immense pleasure to present this book to readers around the world. At this moment, I want to express my gratitude to everyone involved in this achievement.

First and foremost, I would like to express my gratitude to my parents and my family: Mrs Manjiri, Ms Sneha, and Master Shreyas, as well as my brother Milind and his family—Mrs. Mrunal, Ms Shruti, and Master Sushrut. I truly appreciate the encouragement and unwavering support they provide, and I cherish all the moments we share.

I would like to thank my Advisory Mind Performance Coach, Dr. Manjunath M S, for inspiring me to write a book that establishes authority in the IT industry.

I am grateful to my manager, Rajesh Nagarajan, and sector leader, Utkarsh Choubey, for entrusting me with the role of Skills Enablement Leader at the sector level. This opportunity has allowed me to gain a deeper understanding of the needs of both the organization and its employees regarding skill development and career growth.

I would like to sincerely thank Sudhir Agashe and Shirish Patwardhan for reviewing my manuscript and endorsing my book with their insightful comments.

I am thankful to Charith Aryan and his team at Notion Press Publishing for their proactive efforts in bringing this book to life. Their positive approach made the process very seamless.

I would like to thank all my friends, relatives, well-wishers, and all of you – the readers across the globe, for whom I will always take extra steps to give you more. Thank you!!!

Sincerely Yours,

Mohan V Borgaonkar

About the Author

Mohan V. Borgaonkar is a senior leader at a multinational company, possessing extensive experience in cross-cultural, multi-geographic global delivery with distributed teams and worldwide stakeholders. He is a self-motivated professional with excellent leadership skills and holds an engineering degree in Electronics and Telecommunication from Pune University.

Mohan began his career in the electronics industry before transitioning to the IT sector. He has undertaken various roles, including Technical Leader, Project Manager, Business Area Manager, and Senior Functional Leader. Throughout his career, he has worked with consulting IT clients across multiple domains, including HR, Finance, Services, and CIO.

Mohan has received numerous recognition awards, such as Service Excellence, Eminence, Bravo, and Pulling All Together.

With rich experience in global project delivery, Mohan has also served as a Skills Enablement Leader, developing a deep understanding of organizational skill needs and employee aspirations. His insights and experiences have culminated in a book aimed at helping IT professionals worldwide advance their careers in the industry.

In addition to his professional accomplishments, Mohan is a multi-talented artist. He is a musician, arranger for musical programs, flutist, and harmonium player. He is also an avid writer and poet, expressing his sensitive perspective through his literary works.